Mark Water

THE BIBLE

made simple

AMG
Publishers

God's Word is our highest calling.

AMG Publishers
6815 Shallowford Road
Chattanooga, Tennessee 37421

Copyright © 2002 John Hunt Publishing Ltd
Text © 2002 Mark Water
Reprinted 2003

ISBN 0-89957-427-0

Designed by Andrew Milne Design

Printed in China.

Picture Acknowledgement:
Mr Victor Fletcher - p25, p87, p175

Contents

A guide to illuminate

A newcomer to the Bible may be compared to a visitor to an ancient city. The tourist will enjoy the beauty and grace of the old buildings and streets, and will sense the spirit of the place, but to understand the city – the story behind it – he needs a spoken or written guide. Such a guide may even enlighten someone who lives in the city, and is familiar with it.

Similarly with the Bible. It is not necessary to know anything about the background and composition of the Bible to find it challenging and inspiring, and to meet God through its words. But a guide helps to clarify, to illuminate and make accessible much that might otherwise be missed or misunderstood.

The Bible Made Simple aims to be one such guide. It begins by explaining the basic facts about the 66-book library, giving a brief introduction to each book. The reliability of the Bible has been confirmed by numerous archeological discoveries. A survey of the relevance of some of the more important of these now follows. There then follows information about the writing of the Bible and its translation through the centuries. There then follows one "fascinating feature" from each of the Bible books, indicating the treasure that is to be unearthed in every part of the Bible. To enable the reader to have an overview of the complete Bible, the key events in the history of the Israelites and of the life of Christ and the early Church are given. This section includes lists of and explanations about some of the topics found scattered throughout the Bible. This is a handy place to look up, for example, some fact about a particular king of Israel, or the various covenants that are mentioned in the Old Testament and the New Testament.

Many of the more perplexing Bible customs are also cited and explained and the volume concludes with some studies on one of the most mysterious topics in the Bible: Bible symbols.

The Bible Made Simple can only offer a sample of the cornucopia of facts and ideas found in the pages of the Bible. It is hoped that it may encourage the reader to explore further.

Erat qdam
publica
nus no
mine zacheus &
rat cupiens uidere
thm. & qr pusil
lus stature erat
nu potuit eum
uidere p[re]turba:
ideo ascendit in
arbore ut sic eu
uideret transeunt.

Erat iste sig
nificat il
los q p[er]
uirtute humili
tatis oia t[er]rena
r temporalia ppt
xpm relinqu[er]es
ascendut in ar
borem. i. altitu
dine intrauit
transferut se ad
religione. ut ita
clarius r euiden
tius celestia pos
sint contemplari

Cum ap
propin
quass[et],
ihc ierosolimis
r uenisset beth
phage ad mon
tem oliueti: tunc
misit duos dis
c[ipu]los dicens eis.
ite i castellu q[uo]d
uol e r statim inue
nietis asina alli
gata r pullu cu
ea. Soluite r ad
ducite m[ichi]. r[eliqua].

Asina et
pullus
in deos
r gentiles signi
ficant. pasina
alligata signan
t[ur] iudei q[ui] simi
lit[er] peccor[um] r c[er]ta
circul[ex]i uelamine iniuor ob
cecati q p[re]dicati
one aplor[um] nisi
paucissimi po
tuert ad fide co
uerti. p pullu
asine signant[ur]
gentiles q ala[cri]
ter r cu gaudio

1   CONTENTS OF THE BIBLE LIBRARY

Introduction

You probably know that Protestants and Catholics have different Bibles. But how did this come about? And what value do Protestants place on the books that are not in their Bibles, but are in the Apocrypha? All this will now become clear for you.

The books of the Bible do not appear in the order in which they were written. The rationale behind the grouping of the biblical books in our printed Bibles is now explained.

The Bible is made up of more than half a dozen different types of literature. Some of it is presented as a reliable historical record, as Luke himself claims of his own writings, but other parts of the Bible are in the form of poetry or are parables and were never meant to be thought of in a literal way. The different types of biblical literature are listed.

If you want to read or study a Bible book with which you are not familiar, it is helpful to begin with a simple overview of the whole book. Very short summaries of all the Old and New Testament books are therefore given. These descriptions of Bible books will give the reader an increased appreciation of the whole Bible.

Opening the Bible library

Biblia

When you open a Bible you enter a library of 66 books. 39 books make up the Old Testament and 27 books make up the New Testament.

But what does the word "Bible" mean? The word "Bible" comes from the Greek word *biblia* ("books"). The shortened form of *biblia* is *biblos* ("book"). This refers to the inner bark of the papyrus reed from which paper was made in ancient times. This paper was made into scrolls on which people wrote.

Various writers, such as the authors to two apocryphal books, Ecclesiasticus and 1 Maccabees, refer to the books of the Old Testament as "the books," or, "the holy books." By the fifth century AD the whole of the Bible was known as "the Divine Library" and was called *Bibliotheca Divina* by Jerome.

Scripture

The New Testament refers to the Old Testament, not just as a collection of books, but as "the scriptures."

Jesus called the Old Testament "the Scriptures." He said to the chief priests, "Have you never read in the Scriptures" (Matthew 21:42), and then proceeded to quote from Psalm 118:22, 23.

Jesus' followers called the Old Testament "the Scriptures." Two of Jesus' disciples on their walk to Emmaus "asked each other, 'Were not our hearts burning within us while he talked with us on the road and opened the Scriptures to us?'" *Luke 24:32*

Paul referred to the Old Testament as:

- "The holy Scripture" (2 Timothy 3:15)
- "The Holy Scriptures" (Romans 1:2)
- "The very words of God" (Romans 3:2)

Peter even refers to Paul's writings as "the other Scriptures" (2 Peter 3:16).

The word "scripture," in Greek *gramma*, means document or writing. The New Testament uses the phrase "the Scriptures" most often to refer to the whole of the Old Testament which it considered to be a collection of sacred writings.

"Old Testament" and the "New Testament"

By the end of the second century AD the term "Old Testament" was used to refer to the Hebrew Bible, and the term "New Testament" to refer to the Christian Scripture. The first person to use the phrase *Novum Testamentum* (New Testament) was an early Latin father, Tertullian, at the beginning of the third century.

The word "testament" in the phrase "Old Testament," or "New Testament" means "covenant." So it would be accurate to refer to the Old Testament and the New Testament as the "Old Covenant," and the "New Covenant." The word "covenant" is a continuation of the Old Testament name for the law of Moses. Josiah rediscovered "the Book of the Covenant…in the temple of the LORD" (2 Kings 23:2).

THE PROTESTANT OLD TESTAMENT

Roman Catholic Bibles and the Protestant Bibles are different.

The 39 Old Testament books in the Protestant Bible are the same as the 39 books in the Hebrew Bible.

The Old Testament can be divided into the following three categories:

Historical	Poetical	Prophetic
GENESIS	JOB	ISAIAH
EXODUS	PSALMS	JEREMIAH
LEVITICUS	PROVERBS	LAMENTATIONS
NUMBERS	ECCLESIASTES	EZEKIEL
DEUTERONOMY	SONG OF SOLOMON	DANIEL
JOSHUA		HOSEA
JUDGES		JOEL
RUTH		AMOS
1 AND 2 SAMUEL		OBADIAH
1 AND 2 KINGS		JONAH
1 AND 2 CHRONICLES		MICAH
EZRA		NAHUM
NEHEMIAH		HABAKKUK
ESTHER		ZEPHANIAH
		HAGGAI
		ZECHARIAH
		MALACHI

The Roman Catholic Old Testament

In addition to the 39 books of the Hebrew Bible Roman Catholics include 12 more books which they call deuterocanonical books, and which Protestants refer to as "The Old Testament Apocrypha."

12 Deuterocanonical books

- Tobit
- Judith
- Additions to the book of Esther
- Wisdom of Solomon
- Ecclesiasticus, or the Wisdom of Jesus Son of Sirach
- Baruch
- The Letter of Jeremiah
- The additions to the book of Daniel
  The prayer of Azariah and the Song of the Three Jews, or the Song of the Three Children
- Susanna
- Bel and the Dragon
- 1 Maccabees
- 2 Maccabees

Apocrypha, Septuagint, canon

Apocrypha

Some Protestants, such as Anglicans and Lutherans, treated the Old Testament Apocrypha as sub-scriptural, but did not entirely reject it, while Calvinists totally rejected it. According to the *Thirty-Nine Articles* (of the Church of England), these books, "(as Jerome says) the Church does read for example of life and instruction in manners; but does not apply them to establish any doctrine" (Article Two). Martin Luther did not believe that they were equal with sacred scripture, but he thought of them as "useful and good reading."

The word "apocrypha" comes from the Greek word *apokryphos* ("hidden" or "obscure.") This word is a technical one which refers to the relationship of certain books to the Old Testament canon. The word came to refer to the books which were "withdrawn" from being read in public, although they might be read for private edification. The Old Testament Apocrypha refers to the 12 books which were written between the end of the Old Testament and the beginning of the New Testament.

Septuagint

In the third century BC Jewish translators made a very famous translation of their Hebrew scriptures into Greek, which became known as the Septuagint and was used by the Jews in the first century AD. Over the centuries other books were added to the Septuagint.

Jamnia

At a meeting at Jamnia in AD 90 Hebrew rabbis affirmed that only the traditional books of the Hebrew Scriptures should be regarded as Scripture and that all the additional books should be thrown out. Rabbi Akiba stated the position most bluntly: "He who reads the outside books shall have no place in the world to come."

Council of Trent

Some Christians, such as the early Greek-speaking church used the Septuagint and some of the apocryphal books. At the time of the Reformation the Protestants made it clear that the Old Testament Apocrypha was in no way part of Scripture. Roman Catholics, on the other hand, at the Council of Trent, 1546, accepted all of the Old Testament Apocrypha on a par with the rest of the Hebrew Bible, except for 1 and 2 Esdras and the Prayer of Manasseh.

The Orthodox Church

The Orthodox Church (Russian and Greek) have an even larger Old Testament canon than the Roman Catholics. They accept all the books which are accepted by the Roman Catholics as well as:

- 1 Esdras
- The Prayer of Manasseh
- 3 and 4 Maccabees
- Psalm 151

The canon

In literature, the word "canon" refers to a collection of writings which is considered authoritative.

The word "canon" comes from the Greek word *kanon* ("cane" or "reed"). It referred to a carpenter's rule as this was made out of a reed. This rule gave a standard measurement and so set the standard or norm. In the Christian Church, since the fourth century, the word *kanon* has been used to refer to the books which are regarded as Holy Scripture.

The books which today are included in our canon of the New Testament were the ones which were regarded as authoritative by the first leading Christians. The first formal declaration of the New Testament canon was made by the eastern church in 367 in Athanasius' 39th Paschal Letter. The western church agreed the same list of books in 397 at the Council of Carthage.

The 27 New Testament books are divided into the following three categories.

THE 27 NEW TESTAMENT BOOKS			
History	*Letters*		*Prophecy*
MATTHEW	ROMANS	TITUS	REVELATION
MARK	1 CORINTHIANS	PHILEMON	
LUKE	2 CORINTHIANS	HEBREWS	
JOHN	GALATIANS	JAMES	
ACTS	EPHESIANS	1 PETER	
	PHILIPPIANS	2 PETER	
	COLOSSIANS	1 JOHN	
	1 THESSALONIANS	2 JOHN	
	2 THESSALONIANS	3 JOHN	
	1 TIMOTHY	JUDE	
	2 TIMOTHY		

The inspiration of the Bible: Chapter and verse

The New Testament Apocrypha

During the early Christian era over 100 books were written which claimed to be written by an apostle or to contain information about Jesus and the apostles, but which are not included in our New Testament. These books are known as the New Testament Apocrypha.

In the fourth century these books were decisively rejected as being part of the New Testament. Since the exact bounds of the New Testament was then acknowledged no other books have been added.

A divine library

While Roman Catholics, Orthodox and

Below: The earliest surviving fragment of a Christian gospel.

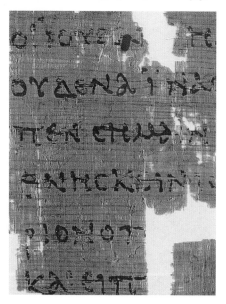

Protestants disagree about the status of the deuterocanonical books of the Old Testament, they agree about the inspiration of both the Old Testament and New Testament.

The inspiration of the Bible refers to the influence God had over its original authors so that nothing erroneous was included. Christians believe in both the human authorship of the Bible and in its divine inspiration.

The Old Testament

The Old Testament claims that its pages record God's revelation. Over 4,000 times the Old Testament says, "Thus says the Lord," as it specifically makes clear that its origin is from God.

David

David asserted, "The Spirit of the LORD spoke through me; his word was on my tongue." *2 Samuel 23:2*

Jeremiah

God told the prophet Jeremiah, "I have put my words in your mouth." *Jeremiah 1:9*

Ezekiel

Ezekiel received this instruction from God, "You must speak my words." *Ezekiel 2:7*

Peter

Peter claims that God was the ultimate author of the Old Testament: "Above all you must understand that no prophecy

of Scripture came about by the prophet's own interpretation. For prophecy never had its origin in the will of men, but men spoke from God as they were carried along by the Holy Spirit."
2 Peter 1:20, 21

God-breathed

"All Scripture is God-breathed and is useful for teaching, rebuking, correcting and training in righteousness, so that the man of God may be thoroughly equipped for every good work." *2 Timothy 3:16, 17*

The point the Bible writers make is that because the Bible is inspired by God it can be trusted.

The order of the books in the New Testament

The books of the New Testament in our Bibles do not appear in the order in which they were written. For many of the letters in the New Testament were written before the four Gospels.

The four Gospels give us four portraits of the life of Jesus and the Acts naturally follows on from them with its record of the formation and history of the activities of the early Christian church.

21 letters then follow which give teaching about how Christ's first followers were to live and how they were to behave and what they were to believe. The first 13 of these letters are traditionally thought to have come from the pen of Paul the apostle. The following eight non-Pauline letters,

written by five authors, James, Peter, John, Jude, and the author of Hebrews, deal firmly with the problems which false teachers caused the Church.

The New Testament is rounded off with a totally different kind of book. The book of Revelation is in the apocalyptic mold and was most probably written to encourage persecuted Christians.

Chapter divisions

The present chapter divisions in our Bibles were originally inserted in 1205 by Stephen Langton, when he was a professor in Paris and before he became Archbishop of Canterbury. He placed them into a Vulgate edition of the Bible. These chapter divisions were first used by the Jews in 1330 in a manuscript of the Hebrew Old Testament and a printed edition in 1516. These chapter divisions were introduced into the Greek manuscripts of the New Testament at the beginning of the fifteenth century.

Verse divisions

The first Bible to divide the text into verses was published in 1560 and became known as the Geneva Bible. It was organized by William Whittingham of Geneva and had Miles Coverdale as one of its translators. The actual verse divisions were made by a Parisian printer of Greek New Testaments, Robert Estienne.

The chapter divisions and verse divisions are handy for reference purposes but are not divinely inspired.

Types of literature in the Bible

Types of literature

A wide variety of different types of literature is found in the pages of the Bible:

- Allegory
- Biography
- Drama
- Exposition
- History
- Hymns
- Law
- Letters
- Oratory
- Parables
- Philosophy
- Poetry
- Prophecy
- Proverbs
- Sermons
- Stories
- Typology
- Wisdom literature

Poetry in the Old Testament

A great deal of the wisdom literature in the Old Testament, Job, Psalms, Proverbs, Ecclesiastes, Song of Solomon, is in the form of poetry. All of the Psalms, the book of Lamentations and the Song of Solomon, and most of the book of Job, Proverbs and Ecclesiastes is poetry.

In addition to that, the oracles in the prophetic books are also in poetic form. Some prayers are also in the form of poetry, such as Jonah's (Jonah 2:2-9) and Habakkuk's (Habakkuk 3:2-19).

The narrative books of the Old Testament also contain some passages of poetry. The three curses in the account of the fall in Genesis 3:14-19, the Song of the Sea in Exodus 15:1-18, the oracle of Balaam in Numbers 23 and 24, and the Song of Moses, Deuteronomy 32:1-43, and the Blessing of Moses in Deuteronomy 33:2-29 are all in the form of poetry.

Old Testament poetry
Rhyme and rhythm

Unlike a great deal of English-language poetry, rhyme is rarely used in Hebrew poetry.

However, there is a great deal of rhythm in Hebrew poetry. Rhythm of sound is achieved by recurring patterns on stressed syllables on a line of poetry. The most well known of these is the dirge meter, so called because it is often used in laments.

> "How deserted / lies / the city, once so full / of people." *Lamentations 1:1*

In this instance the stressed syllables are in the 3:2 pattern. A sequence of alternating clauses with this pattern gives the effect of an elegy.

Parallelism

This literary device was the one most favored by Hebrew poets. It took three main forms:

- Complete parallelism
- Incomplete parallelism, and
- "Staircase" parallelism

Complete parallelism

Complete parallelism describes two lines of poetry where the poet either repeats the exact idea or a contrasting or opposite idea in the following line. Isaiah 1:3 is an example of this:

> But Israel does not know,
> my people do not understand.

Here the words "Israel" and "my people," and "does not know" and "do not understand" are used to express an identical idea. A further example comes in Isaiah 44:22:

> I have swept away your offenses
> like a cloud,
> your sins like the morning mist.

Antithetic

An example of *antithetic* parallelism, where the poet expresses one idea in one line, and the opposite idea in the following line comes in Proverbs 15:20:

> A wise man brings joy to his father,
> but a foolish man despises his
> mother.

Emblematic

Another type of parallelism, called *emblematic* parallelism, repeats an idea in symbolic or figurative terms. An example of this also comes in the book of Proverbs, 26:21.

> As charcoal to embers and as
> wood to fire,
> so is a quarrelsome man for
> kindling strife.

Incomplete parallelism

Where the Hebrew poet employs incomplete parallelism he does not repeat all of his first idea. An example of this is taken from Psalm 1:5:

> (1) Therefore the wicked
> (2) will not stand
> (3) in judgment,
> (1) nor sinners
> (3) in the assembly of the righteous.

In this instance, the second line of the verse repeats the first and the third element of line one, but not the second element.

"Staircase" parallelism

Yet another type of parallelism is called climactic, step-parallelism, or staircase parallelism, as comes in Psalm 92:9:

> (1) For surely your enemies,
> (2) O Lord,
> (1) surely your enemies
> (3) will perish;
> (1) all evildoers
> (3) will be scattered.

In this instance the poet does not repeat the second element of his first line in the second line. Rather, he emphasizes the idea with a third element (3), which he repeats at the end of his sentence.

Summary of each Old Testament book
PART 1: GENESIS THRU' ECCLESIASTES

GENESIS
Beginnings
After the account of God's creation of the world, Genesis relates how Noah built an ark to escape from the great flood. Genesis also tells the story of Abraham, Isaac, Jacob and Joseph.

EXODUS
Rescued
Exodus is the book about the ten terrible plagues, and the Israelites' great escape from the land of Egypt, under the gifted leadership of Moses.

LEVITICUS
Holy, holy, holy
Leviticus takes its title from the priests and the tribe of Levi. This book is about God's holiness. It explains how God's rescued and redeemed people should worship, serve and obey him.

NUMBERS
In the desert
What should have been a two-week journey for the Israelites, to arrive in the land God had promised to give them, turned into 40 years of wandering around in the desert, and all because of their disobedience to God.

DEUTERONOMY
Remember, remember
As the people of Israel are at last poised to enter the land God had promised to give them, their leader, Moses, counsels them to remember God, and never

disobey him, but be blessed by obeying him.

JOSHUA
The Promised Land
Joshua becomes the very capable leader of the people of Israel. This book describes the problems they faced during their seven years of conquest, and the settling of the 12 tribes of Israel in the pagan land of Canaan.

JUDGES
Turn back to God
The people of Israel ignore and displease God, time and again. But when they do turn back to God they are forgiven. Their 17 judges, who include Gideon and Samson, act as their legal, political and spiritual rulers.

RUTH
True devotion
Set in the time of the Judges, here is a touching story about a non-Jewish widow, Ruth. She elects to leave her own country to live with and devote herself to her widowed Jewish mother-in-law, Naomi, in Bethlehem.

1 & 2 SAMUEL
The king maker
Samuel, Israel's last judge and first great prophet, anoints young David to be king elect. Saul is eaten alive with jealousy of David. This portrait of Israel's most famous king shows him warts and all!

1 & 2 KINGS
The great division
Solomon and the building of the Temple in Jerusalem take the center stage in 1 Kings. Then Solomon's divided loyalties towards God are reflected in the break-up of the 12 tribes of Israel into two kingdoms, Israel and Judah.

1 & 2 CHRONICLES
King David the Great
1 Chronicles records the spiritual significance of King David's reign, as the writer sets out to encourage the Jews who had returned from exile.
2 Chronicles concentrates on the building and glory of Solomon's temple.

EZRA
Back to Jerusalem
The book of Ezra records the return of the Jews to Jerusalem after their 70 years of exile in Babylon. The first 50,000 return under Zerubbabel's leadership: 2,000 return with Ezra who rebuilds the spiritual life of the Jews.

NEHEMIAH
Rebuilding for God
Some 13 years after Ezra, Nehemiah led the third and last return of the Jews from Babylon to Jerusalem. Under his courageous leadership the shattered walls of Jerusalem were rebuilt, despite all the opposition.

ESTHER
A moment for courage
Esther gives us our only glimpse into the life of the exiled Jews who stayed behind in Persia. Although God is not mentioned by name in the book, his protecting hand is clearly seen in this moving story of Esther's courage.

JOB
Suffering humanity
Job's four so-called comforters are all wide of the mark with their explanation about why devastating personal tragedy should strike Job. The correct response to suffering is seen in the last chapter of the book when Job worships God.

PSALMS
Songs of praise
The Psalms were Israel's hymn-book; they became the devotional guide for the people of Israel. Above all, they give praise to God for who he is.

PROVERBS
True wisdom
A collection of some 200 inspired, short, pithy proverbs. They give clear moral teaching, and show in very practical ways how to please God.

ECCLESIASTES
All is vanity
Ecclesiastes seeks for the key to the meaning of life. Vanity, mentioned 37 times, the futile emptiness of trying to be happy apart from God, is everywhere. This book shows how life only makes sense as one stands in awe of God.

PART 2: SONG OF SOLOMON THRU' MALACHI

SONG OF SOLOMON
Love comes from God
At one level this is a love song written by Solomon. At another level it is a picture of Israel as God's bride, and the church as Jesus Christ's bride.

ISAIAH
Salvation
The prophet Isaiah warned Judah not to trust in military alliances but in God's powers. Isaiah taught that salvation, physical and spiritual, only comes from God, not from man.

JEREMIAH
Come back to God
For 40 years, the prophet Jeremiah called the people of Israel back to God. He had to battle against idolatry, moral decadence and corrupt worship. For his pains, he is imprisoned and beaten and treated as a traitor.

LAMENTATIONS
Facing devastation
Jeremiah cries from the depths of his heart over the destruction of Jerusalem. He confesses Judah's sin, and in the middle of total disaster he recalls how good and faithful God is.

EZEKIEL
A new heart
This man of visions comforts the Israelites in their Babylonian exile by reminding them that God will one day restore their land to them.

DANIEL
God rules
Daniel shows his outstanding faith in God in the lions' den, and rises to become an influential statesman. The story encourages the exiled Jews in Babylon, by emphasizing how God rules over the destinies of nations.

HOSEA
I loved you
The prophet Hosea's message was given to the northern kingdom of Israel. Hosea's own personal tragedies with the adulterous wife Gomer mirror Israel's spiritual faithlessness to God.

JOEL
Locusts
The prophet Joel's message was given to the southern kingdom of Judah. From a recent terrible locust plague, Joel illustrates God's coming day of judgment. Joel urges his hearers to repent before it is too late.

AMOS
A bright future
To the prosperous northern kingdom of Israel Amos delivers his unpopular message. He speaks against their corrupt business practices and phoney religion. God's judgment is close but the book ends on a note of hope.

OBADIAH
Future hope
The Edomites invaded Judah just as

Judah was being ransacked by the Babylonians. Obadiah prophesies Edom's downfall.

JONAH
The reluctant preacher
Jonah tries to avoid God's call to preach to the wicked people of Nineveh, but God insists – he sends a storm and a large fish to stop Jonah running away. Jonah learns the lesson that God loves people outside the Jewish race, as the wicked people of Nineveh repent..

MICAH
Walking with God
Micah is appalled by the oppression of the poor by the rich, and the corrupt judges and religious leaders. He predicts that God will judge the people of Judah for this, but he ends with a message of comfort and hope.

NAHUM
God's judgment
Nahum the prophet predicts the fall of Nineveh, the arrogant capital city of Assyria. Nineveh's destruction is seen as God's judgment on the Assyrians' neglect of God and on their harshness towards other nations.

HABAKKUK
A cry of faith
"Why do the wicked and cruel Babylonians go unpunished?" asks the prophet Habakkuk. He finds his answer in God's goodness and wisdom, and in

the fact that nothing can ultimately thwart God's plans.

ZEPHANIAH
The day of the Lord
The prophet Zephaniah emphasizes the need for the people of Judah to turn away from idolatry, and focuses on their need for personal and spiritual revival. If they repent, God promises to bless them.

HAGGAI
Finish the temple
The Jews are now settled back in Jerusalem, but the rebuilding of the temple is being neglected. Haggai galvanizes them into action as he encourages the people to renew their trust in the Lord.

ZECHARIAH
The Messiah will come
Like Haggai, the prophet Zechariah urges the people of Jerusalem to complete the rebuilding of the temple. In a series of visions, Zechariah stresses that they must be a holy people. He is certain that the Messiah will come.

MALACHI
Return and repent
The temple has been rebuilt, and yet the people of Jerusalem still displease God. They worship idols, crush the poor and marry pagans. Malachi urges them to repent and to return to their God, the God of love and justice.

Summary of each New Testament book
MATTHEW THRU' TITUS

MATTHEW
God's Messiah
Matthew uses numerous Old Testament references to show how Jesus Christ is indeed the long-awaited Messiah. Matthew records a great deal of Jesus' teaching, especially about the kingdom of heaven.

MARK
The suffering Servant
Mark emphasizes that Jesus Christ came as a servant who suffered his death on the cross on behalf of the world. Mark also takes great care to show that Jesus Christ is the Son of God.

LUKE
Jesus Christ's compassion
To Dr Luke, Jesus Christ is the Savior of the world. Luke portrays Jesus Christ's great concern for all people, especially the poor, the ill, the outsiders, the children, the helpless and the rejects of society.

JOHN
The Son of God
John sets out to present the life, death, resurrection and teaching of Jesus Christ in such a way that people will come to place their own faith in the Son of God, whose gift to them is eternal life.

ACTS
The worldwide mission
Dr Luke shows how the first Christians (especially Peter and Paul) lived, how they spoke about Jesus Christ, under the direction and power of the Holy Spirit and how they spread the Christian message as far as Rome.

ROMANS
Peace with God
In a magisterial treatise on the Christian message, Paul shows how God accepts us not because we have been good but because he loves us. All we do is place our grateful trust in Jesus Christ.

1 CORINTHIANS
Love is the greatest
The church at Corinth was full of spiritual life. But it also had its fair share of Christians who were behaving in very un-Christian ways. Paul writes to encourage the first and correct the second.

2 CORINTHIANS
A new creation
False teachers frequently arrived after Paul left. Paul refutes their teachings, and in doing so he relates the tough experiences and persecutions he has faced as a follower of Jesus Christ.

GALATIANS
Only one gospel
Paul taught that the only way to God is through trust in Jesus Christ. Paul reserves some of his most blunt words for those Galatian Christians who were being wooed away from this basic Christian teaching.

EPHESIANS
Spiritual blessings
Paul rehearses the wonderful spiritual privileges which God has made available to all Christians – forgiveness, God's acceptance of us, grace, the sealing of the Holy Spirit, etc. – before he says, "Be united to one another."

PHILIPPIANS
Rejoice in the Lord
Paul, under the shadow of the death sentence, writes from his prison cell, and encourages the Philippian Christians to take heart and rejoice in the Lord, as they face persecution and false teachers.

COLOSSIANS
Christ is supreme
When Paul heard that some Christians at Colossae were polluting and diluting Christian teaching with dangerous false teaching, he dashed off this letter, to emphasize that Christ alone is supreme in everything.

1 THESSALONIANS
A follow-up letter
As a result of Paul's preaching at Thessalonica some people became followers of Christ and they remained dear in Paul's heart. He writes this letter to encourage them in their new-found faith.

2 THESSALONIANS
Jesus will return
False teachers had been saying that "the day of Christ" had already taken place, and so were upsetting the new Christians at Thessalonica. Paul reminds them that certain events will take place before Jesus' return.

1 TIMOTHY
How to be a pastor
The ageing Paul writes to encourage his young protégé Timothy. Paul touches on how to run a church fellowship, how to worship and the kind of people church leaders should be.

2 TIMOTHY
My dear son
2 Timothy is Paul's last letter. It is his last will and testament to his spiritual son Timothy. Paul emphasizes the need for Timothy to lead a godly life and to preach the gospel faithfully.

TITUS
Live for God
Paul writes to advise the young minister Titus, who is helping the new Christian church on the island of Crete. He advises about the appointment of church leaders and how all church members must live lives pleasing to God.

Philemon thru' Revelation

PHILEMON
Your runaway slave
This is the only private letter of Paul to survive. He urges his good friend Philemon to receive back his runaway slave Onesimus, since he has now become a follower of Jesus Christ.

HEBREWS
Jesus Christ is the best
The unknown author of this letter emphasizes that Jesus Christ is far superior to the Old Testament prophets and priests. To strengthen the faith of some wavering Jewish Christians Jesus Christ is presented as the only Savior.

JAMES
Faith and works
James challenges his readers to live out a true Christian faith and so bring honor and credit to Jesus. He emphasizes that Christians should both have faith in God and be encouraged in doing good deeds.

1 PETER
Faith under attack
The storm clouds of persecution are gathering. Peter, the rugged fisherman, pens 1 Peter in order to strengthen the Christian faith of those about to walk through the fires of persecution.

2 PETER
False teachers
To counteract malign false teaching Peter urges his readers to grow into mature followers of Jesus as he reminds them of the timeless truth of the Christian faith.

1 JOHN
God is love
1 John tells people who had become followers of Jesus Christ how to be sure about their Christian faith.

2 JOHN
Error refuted
The readers of 2 John are told to hang on to true Christian teaching and not to give an inch to the false teachers.

3 JOHN
Fellowship with Christians
3 John encourages hospitality for traveling Christians as there were then few safe places to stay.

JUDE
Fight for the faith
How do you stop followers of Christ from being led astray by false teachers? Jude says, "become strong in your Christian faith and then you will not be lured away."

REVELATION
The book of visions
With the persecution, imprisonment and killing of Christians being the order of the day, John, exiled on Patmos, writes to inspire Christians to be strong in their faith. His message is that God is still in control.

Bible statistics

In the whole Bible

Shortest chapter
Psalm 117 (2 verses, 33 words)

Longest verse
Esther 8:9 (90 words)

Longest Old Testament book
Psalms, 150 chapters, 2,461 verses

Longest New Testament book
Luke, 24 chapters, 1,151 verses

Longest word in the Bible

Two words in the Bible, both with 18 letters, tie for being the longest words in the Bible

1. Jonath-elem-rechokim
   This is the title to Psalm 56 and means "A dove on distant oaks."
2. Maher-shalal-hash-baz
   The word comes in Isaiah 8:1 and 8:3. It is the name of Isaiah's son, and means "quick to the plunder, swift to the spoil."

	OLD TESTAMENT	NEW TESTAMENT	WHOLE BIBLE
Number of books	39	27	66
Number of chapters	929	260	1,189
Number of verses	23,214	7,959	31,173
Number of words	592,493	181,253	773,746
Number of letters	2,728,100	838,380	3,566,480
Longest chapter	Psalm 119 176 verses	Matthew 26 75 verses	Psalm 119
Middle book	Proverbs	2 Thessalonians	Micah and Nahum
Middle chapter	Job 29	Romans 13 and 14	Psalm 117
Middle verse	2 Chronicles 20:17	Acts 17:17	Psalm 118:8
Shortest book	Obadiah 21 verses	3 John 14 verses, 299 words (2 John has 13 verses but 303 words)	3 John
Shortest verse	1 Chronicles 1:1 Adam, Seth, Enosh	John 11:35 Jesus wept	John 11:35

2 | *YOUR GUIDE TO THE BACKGROUND OF THE BIBLE*

Introduction

There have been countless archeological digs in Bible lands since 1890 when Sir W. M. Flinders Petrie first discovered the significance of stratigraphy (the arrangement of layers of earth indicating differing eras) at Tell-el-Hesi. But do these archeological finds undermine or confirm the reliability of the Bible? And what is so special about the tens of thousands of fragments of manuscripts, which we know as the Dead Sea Scrolls, discovered since 1947 in the Qumran Caves? This chapter attempts to answer these questions.

Have you ever wondered what languages the Bible was originally written in? Or who the writers of the Bible were? Or what can be said about the books of the Bible which are anonymous? These are some of the questions discussed in chapter 2.

The story of the translation and transmission of the Bible from one generation to the next is fascinating. Choosing between the scores of different Bible versions, translations and paraphrases we have today need not be a problem. We are helped when we understand how they came about – the purpose and approach of each translation or paraphrase. And our own Bible study today can be enriched when we compare the translations found in the different versions – one doesn't need to know a word of Greek to benefit from the work of the biblical scholars who translated the Bible.

Right: One of the caves in which the Dead Sea Scrolls were found.

The Bible and archeology:

DISCOVERIES THAT HAVE CONFIRMED THE OLD TESTAMENT

Archeology cannot "prove" that the Bible is true. However, scores of archeological discoveries confirm the accuracy of the Bible record and shed light on many customs of Bible times.

The Moabite Stone

At Dibon, which is three miles north of the River Arnon and which had once been the capital of Mesha, king of Moab, F.A. Cline had his attention drawn by a friendly sheik in 1868 to the protruding top of a black basalt stone. The Moabite Stone, 3 feet 10 inches high, 2 feet wide and 14 inches thick now resides in the Museum of the Louvre, Paris. It is a monument dedicated to the god Chemosh by Mesha, king of Moab, who erected it in about 850 BC.

Before this discovery some scholars had suggested that the information contained in 2 Kings was mistaken because Moab would have been too barren to graze sheep. "Now Mesha king of Moab raised sheep, and he had to supply the king of Israel with a hundred thousand lambs and with the wool of a hundred thousand rams. But after Ahab died, the king of Moab rebelled against the king of Israel." 2 Kings 3:4, 5

Among the 34 lines of alphabetical script on the Moabite Stone it records Mesha's victory over the Israelites in the days of Ahab in the following way: "I am Mesha, King of Moab, the Dibonite… My father ruled over Moab thirty years, and I ruled after my father. And I made this high place to Chemosh [god of Moab] because of the deliverance of Mesha, because he saved me from all the Kings and caused me to see my desire upon all who hated me. Omri, king of Israel, oppressed Moab, and his son [Ahab] after him. I warred against their cities, devoted the spoil to Chemosh, and in Beth-diblathaim sheep raisers I placed."

The Black Obelisk

In 1845 Henry Layard discovered the Black Obelisk as he explored a mound at Nimrud, 20 miles south of Nineveh on the west bank of the Tigris River. In the middle of the ruins of Shalmanezer III's palace he discovered a 6 foot 6 inches tall obelisk which had five small bas-reliefs on each side, which is now in the British Museum in London.

It depicts officials from five different countries with the tribute they brought to Shalmanezer III. 210 lines of cuneiform inscription describe the campaigns and achievements of Shalmanezer III of Assyria, 810–782 BC. On the obelisk Shalmanezer says, "In the eighteenth year of my reign…I received tribute from the inhabitants of Tyre, Sideon, and of Jehu, son of Omri." Later the inscription continues, "The tribute of Jehu, son of Omri: I received from him silver, gold, a golden bowl, a golden vase with pointed bottom, golden goblets, pictures of gold, bars of lead, staffs for the hand of the King, and javelins, I received."

This is the only sculptured relief of

Below: The Moabite Stone which confirms Old Testament accounts of events.

any Israelite king that has ever been found. Jehu has a rounded beard, a leather cap and a sleeveless jacket which identifies him as a prisoner.

Scenes on the obelisk show tribute being paid to the great Assyrian monarch and one panel depicts Jehu bowing before the king in the presence of his officers.

The Sennacherib prism

In 1845 H.A. Layard, while excavating Nineveh, discovered a hexagonal prism (clay inscription) which recorded details of Sennacherib's eight military campaigns. Referring to the invasion of Judah in about 686 BC it says, "As for Hezekiah, the Jew, who did not sumbit to my yoke...I besieged him like a caged bird shut up in his city of Jerusalem."

Sennacherib does not claim to have captured Jerusalem which supports the biblical account of 2 Kings chapters 18 and 19. "That night the angel of the LORD went out and put to death a hundred and eighty-five thousand men in the Assyrian camp." *2 Kings 19:35*

Ancient monarchs seldom recorded reversals or defeats.

Hezekiah's tunnel

When Hezekiah, one of the kings of the southern kingdom of Judah, realized that Sennacherib was about to attack Judah, he decided to make sure that the invaders would have difficulty in finding an adequate water supply. He also took steps to ensure Jerusalem had a good water supply.

He constructed a tunnel from the spring at Gihon (which is now called the Virgin's Fountain) under the city walls and through the rock to the southern end of the city of Jerusalem, to the pool of Siloam. Despite the impending invasion gangs of workmen started from either end. When the tunnel was complete, the spring outside the city was blocked up and the water flowed into the city.

This event is recorded in the Bible in the second book of Chronicles. "When Hezekiah saw that Sennacherib had come and that he intended to make war on Jerusalem, he consulted with his officials and military staff about blocking off the water from the springs outside the city, and they helped him. A large

force of men assembled, and they blocked all the springs and the stream that flowed through the land. 'Why should the king of Assyria come and find plenty of water?' they said." *2 Chronicles 32:2-4*

"As for the other events of Hezekiah's reign, all his achievements and how he made the pool and the tunnel by which he brought water into the city, are they not written in the book of the annals of the kings of Judah?" *2 Kings 20:20*

The Siloam Incription

In 1880 schoolboys were wading in the Pool of Siloam and waded some 19 feet along the 2 foot wide, 6 foot high tunnel. On the east wall they discovered some writing above the waterline which turned out to be six lines of Hebrew.

This inscription is written in the old Hebrew script of the time of Hezekiah and part of the tablet, which is now in the Istanbul Museum, reads:

"Now this is the history of the excavations. While the excavators were still lifting up the pick, each towards his neighbor, and while there were yet three cubits [four and a half feet] to excavate, there was heard the voice of one man calling to his neighbor. On the day the workmen struck, ax against ax, to meet his neighbors, waters flowed from the spring to the [Gihon] Spring to the [Siloam] Pool, a distance of 1,200 cubits [1,800 feet]; and one hundred cubits [150 feet] was the height of the rock above the head of the miners."

Discoveries that have confirmed the New Testament

Pontius Pilate

The theater at Caesarea which goes back to the time of King Herod was excavated between 1959 and 1963 when a Latin inscription bearing the words, "Pontius Pilate, Prefect of Judea" was unearthed.

The politarchs of Thessalonica

Some scholars used to point out that Luke could not be trusted as an accurate historian because the name he gave to the magistrates or officials of the city was "politarch." "They dragged Jason… before the city *officials*" (Acts 17:6). These scholars said that the name "politarch" had not been found in any other Greek literature and so Luke must have been mistaken. However, 17 inscriptions have been found in Thessalonica with the name "politarch" on them.

The most famous one, until a riot in 1876, formed part of the arch of the Vardar Gate. Luke would have seen the inscription as he passed under the arch. It reads, "In the time of Politarchs, Sosipatros, son of Cleopatra…" It listed six city officials who were "politarchs," that is head of the people's assembly.

Inscription from Herod's temple

Paul's final arrest recorded in Acts was sparked by some Jews from Asia who accused Paul of bringing Greeks into the temple area and so defiling the holy place (see Acts 21:27-29).

This biblical incident was confirmed in 1871 when Clermont-Ganneau found an inscription which had once been part of Herod's magnificent temple and marked the boundary line beyond which no Gentiles were allowed to set foot. The inscription, dating from about AD 30 read: "No stranger [Gentile] is to enter within the balustrade round the Temple and enclosure. Whoever is caught doing so will be responsible to himself for his death, which will follow."

How do the Dead Sea Scrolls confirm the Bible?

What was found?

In 1947 young Bedouin shepherds lost a goat in the Judean Desert. During their search they went into one of the caves to the north-west of the Dead Sea, just 13 miles east of Jerusalem. There they found jars filled with ancient scrolls. To start with the Bedouins found seven scrolls. Over the next nine years ten more caves yielded thousands of scroll fragments.

Most of the finds are in the form of fragmented texts, and they have been numbered according to the cave in which they were found.

The 11 caves

Cave 1

Caves 1 and 11 produced the most intact manuscripts. In Cave 1, after the fragments had been assembled, it was discovered that the following seven leather scrolls had been found:

- A complete Isaiah scroll
- A partial Isaiah scroll
- A commentary on the book of Habakkuk, including two chapters of Habakkuk
- The Manual of Discipline, which were the rules for the members of the religious community (Essenes) who lived nearby
- Hymns of thanksgiving
- A Genesis apocryphon (apocryphal stories of some of the patriarchs)
- Wars of the Sons of Light Against the Sons of Darkness (an account of a

war, which may have been real or spiritual, between some Hebrew tribes and some other tribes who lived east of Jordan)

Other caves

After finding such manuscript treasure in Cave 1 a further 270 surrounding caves were carefully searched. Further manuscripts were found in ten other caves.

In Cave 2 fragments from nearly 100 scrolls of the books of Exodus, Leviticus, Numbers, Deuteronomy, Jeremiah, Job, Psalms and Ruth were found.

Cave 3 housed mysterious copper scrolls which gave directions about buried treasure which has never been found.

Cave 4 which was discovered in 1952, produced the largest find consisting of some 15,000 fragments from more than 500 manuscripts. In Cave 4 part of 1

Below: Scroll of Isaiah from the Dead Sea Scrolls.

Samuel, dating back to the third century BC, is the oldest known fragment of any Old Testament book in existence. Among the biblical scrolls found in Cave 4 every book of the Hebrew canon (Old Testament) have been discovered except for the book of Esther.

Caves 5–10 produced a variety of biblical and non-biblical fragments.

Cave 11 housed 48 psalms, 7 of which are non-biblical psalms.

Multiple copies

Among the scrolls, 19 copies of the Book of Isaiah, 25 copies of Deuteronomy and 30 copies of the Psalms have been identified.

In total, fragments from about 825 to 870 separate scrolls have been identified.

Importance of the Dead Sea Scrolls

The biblical scrolls in the Dead Sea Scroll collection are the oldest group of Old Testament manuscripts ever found.

The Isaiah scroll

In Cave 1 two Isaiah scrolls were found and they are regarded as the most famous of the finds among the Dead Sea Scrolls. The first scroll (1QIsa) has the whole of the Hebrew text of the book of Isaiah, while the second Isaiah scroll (1QIsb) has one third of the text.

The first Isaiah scroll has been dated back to the second century BC. Its 17 sheets are 10 inches high and together are 24 feet long. Before this find the oldest Isaiah manuscript was about

1,000 years later – the standard Masoritic Hebrew text. The Masoritic text and the Isaiah scroll from Cave 1 are amazingly alike, so scholars have concluded that this demonstrates the accuracy of the Hebrew text.

The Essenes

Excavations carried out between Cave 4 and the Dead Sea unearthed the ancient ruins of Qumran which were excavated in 1951, 1953–1956 and appear to be connected with the scrolls.

It is probable that the Dead Sea Scrolls were written by the Essenes from about 200 BC – AD 68. The Essenes, referred to by Josephus but not in the New Testament, were a strict Jewish sect, led by an unnamed priest whom they called the "Teacher of Righteousness."

This religious community had used the surrounding 11 caves to house and hide their precious library. Their manuscripts of leather parchment, copper and papyrus were preserved in unique pottery jars which may have been produced specifically for the purpose of storing these manuscripts.

An evaluation of the Dead Sea Scrolls

When William Foxwell Albright saw John C. Trevor's photographs of the scroll of Isaiah from Cave 1 at Qumran in March 1948, he said, "I repeat that in my opinion you have made the greatest manuscript discovery of modern times... certainly the greatest biblical manuscript find...What an incredible find!"

Writing the Bible:
HOW THE BIBLE WAS ORIGINALLY WRITTEN

Languages of the Bible

The Bible was originally written in three languages:

- Hebrew   • Aramaic   • Greek

The Old Testament

Nearly all of the Old Testament was written in Hebrew, a Semitic dialect, which had similarities with Phoenician and Ugaritic dialects.

The only parts of the Old Testament written in Aramaic, which was also a Semitic language, not dissimilar to Hebrew, are:

- Ezra 4:8–6:18
- Ezra 7:12-26
- Daniel 2:4–7:28
- Jeremiah 10:11

The New Testament

All of the New Testament was written in Greek. From archeological discoveries it has been possible to identify the Greek of the New Testament as the Greek used in everyday language in the contemporary world. Today, we call this Greek *Koine* Greek, Common Greek, which is different from classical Greek.

What Wycliffe's Bible translation into English did for the English, Matthew, Mark and all the other writers of the New Testament did for the people of the Roman world.

Hebrew words found in the New Testament

A number of Hebrew words found in the New Testament bear witness to the

Semitic background of the New Testament.

- Allelouia
- Amen
- Genna
- Korban ("gift")
- Koros ("kora" Hebrew 10-12 bushel measure)
- Manna
- Pascha (Passover)
- Sabaoth
- Sabbaton (Sabbath)
- Satanas
- Hyssopos

Aramaic words found in the New Testament

Most of the Aramaic words found in the four Gospels are kept as transliterations from the Aramaic. They are sometimes referred to as the "actual words of Jesus," the *ipsissima verba* of Jesus, as Jesus is most likely to have spoken in Aramaic.

- Abba (father)
- Eloi, Eloi, lama sabachthani? (My God, my God, why have you forsaken me? Matthew 27:46)
- ephphatha (be opened)
- Korbanas (temple treasury)
- Mammonas (Mammon)
- maran atha (Our Lord has come) or marana tha (our Lord, come!)
- Rabbi (my master)
- Rabbouni (my lord)
- raka (fool, empty-headed)
- Sikera (strong drink)
- Talitha koum(i) (little girl, get up!)

Who wrote the letter to the Hebrews?

Was it not Paul?

The *King James Version* of the Bible gives the letter to the Hebrews the title: "The Epistle of Paul the Apostle to the Hebrews". From about AD 400–1600 few people questioned Paul's authorship of this letter.

Problems with Pauline authorship

1. It is anonymous

But few people believe this today. The book is anonymous. The author of this letter is nowhere identified in the letter. If Paul was the author of Hebrews it would be the only New Testament letter of his that does not bear his name, ("Paul, a servant of Christ Jesus, called to be an apostle" Romans 1:1).

2. The letter has no personal greetings

If Paul did write the letter to the Hebrews it would be the only letter we have of his which does not contain personal greetings to his readers, ("Greet Priscilla and Aquila, my fellow-workers in Christ Jesus" Romans 16:3).

3. Paul's direct revelation

In addition to the style of the letter to the Hebrews, which differs from all other New Testament books, there is another major objection to Paul being the author of Hebrews. In Galatians 1:11, 12, Paul wrote, "I want you to know, brothers, that the gospel I preached is not something that man made up. I did not receive it from any

man, nor was I taught it; rather, I received it by revelation from Jesus Christ." Paul insists that the gospel was not communicated to him by another person, but by revelation from Jesus Christ. However, in Hebrews 2:3, the writer of Hebrews says, "this salvation, which was first announced by the Lord, was confirmed to us by those who heard him." Clearly this writer had not received special revelation from the risen Lord.

So who did write Hebrews?

Luther favored Apollos. Other names that have been suggested include Barnabas, Luke, Silvanus and Priscilla. Most Bible scholars today do not know for certain who wrote this letter, and many are content to admit their ignorance in this area, and say with Origen, "who wrote the epistle, in truth, God alone knows."

Who wrote the books of the Bible?

Many of the Bible books clearly state who they were written by. The book which contains the prophecies of Jeremiah opens with these words: "The words of Jeremiah son of Hilkiah, one of the priests at Anathoth in the territory of Benjamin."

Some books of the Bible claim to be written by more than one person. While David wrote more of the psalms than anyone else, the headings in the psalms themselves state that other people also wrote some of the psalms.

- Moses: psalm 90
- Solomon: psalm 72
- Three temple musicians:
  Asaph: 50; 73-83

Ethan: 89
The sons of Korah: 42-49, 84, 85, 87, 88

The book we now know as the book of Psalms is a collection of hymns and prayers, if not a collection of collections of psalms of praise.

Anonymous books
The book of Job does not say who its author was. Bible scholars point out that the one person who did not write this book was Job, on the grounds that he lived in the land of Uz, Job 1:1, and so was not an Israelite. But the book of Job often used the special Israelite name for God, Yahweh, (or LORD, in the NIV.)

BIBLE BOOKS AND THEIR AUTHORS

Bible book	Traditional author	Bible book	Traditional author
OLD TESTAMENT		Habakkuk	Habakkuk
Genesis	Moses	Zephaniah	Zephaniah
Exodus	Moses	Haggai	Haggai
Leviticus	Moses	Zechariah	Zechariah
Numbers	Moses	Malachi	Malachi
Deuteronomy	Moses	**NEW TESTAMENT**	
Joshua	Joshua	Matthew	Matthew
Judges	Unknown	Mark	Mark
Ruth	Unknown	Luke	Luke
1 and 2 Samuel	Unknown	John	John
1 and 2 Kings	Unknown	Acts	Luke
1 and 2 Chronicles	Unknown	Romans	Paul
Ezra	Ezra	1 Corinthians	Paul
Nehemiah	Nehemiah	2 Corinthians	Paul
Esther	Esther	Galatians	Paul
Job	Unknown	Ephesians	Paul
Psalms	David & others	Philippians	Paul
Proverbs	Solomon & others	Colossians	Paul
		1 Thessalonians	Paul
Ecclesiastes	Solomon	2 Thessalonians	Paul
Song of Solomon	Solomon	1 Timothy	Paul
Isaiah	Isaiah	2 Timothy	Paul
Jeremiah	Jeremiah	Titus	Paul
Lamentations	Jeremiah	Philemon	Paul
Ezekiel	Ezekiel	Hebrews	Unknown
Daniel	Daniel	James	James
Hosea	Hosea	1 Peter	Peter
Joel	Joel	2 Peter	Peter
Amos	Amos	1 John	John
Obadiah	Obadiah	2 John	John
Jonah	Jonah	3 John	John
Micah	Micah	Jude	Jude
Nahum	Nahum	Revelation	John

Translating the Bible:
THE HISTORY OF THE TRANSLATION OF THE ENGLISH BIBLE

This history of the translation of the Bible into English has two major pivotal points:

- the translations of the Bible into the vernacular, and,
- the translation of the *English Revised Version* and the *American Standard Version* (1901)

Translations into the vernacular

One of the driving forces of the Bible translators before, and at the time of the Reformation, was to produce a Bible that could be read and easily understood by everyone. They translated the Bible into the vernacular, the standard language of a country or locality. The outstanding example of this is Luther's German translation of the Bible.

The *English Revised Version* and the *American Standard Version*

Since the turn of the nineteenth century, following the publications of the *English Revised Version* and the *American Standard Version* there has been a flood of Bible translations. Over 100 different English translations of the Bible were made in the twentieth century.

Early Bible versions

Anglo-Saxon versions of the Bible, or parts of the Bible, were made by Caedmon, Bede and Aldhelm in the seventh century, and Alfred the Great in the ninth century, and Aelfric in the eleventh century. English bards put the pslams into regular poetic form.

SOURCES OF EARLY ENGLISH BIBLE VERSIONS		
Version	*Date*	*Source*
Wycliffe	1380	Latin *Vulgate*
Tyndale	1525-30	Latin *Vulgate*, Greek and Hebrew Manuscripts
Coverdale	1535	Latin *Vulgate*, Luther's *German Bible*, Tyndale's version
Matthew's Bible	1537	Greek and Hebrew manuscripts, Tyndale's version
Great Bible	1540	Tyndale's version, *Matthew's Bible*
Geneva Bible	1560	Tyndale's version, *Great Bible*
Bishops' Bible	1568	*Great Bible*
Rheims	1582	Latin *Vulgate*, Greek and Hebrew manuscripts
Douay	1602	Latin *Vulgate*, Greek and Hebrew manuscripts
King James Version	1611	Greek and Hebrew manuscripts, Tyndale's version, Coverdale's version, *Geneva Bible*, *Bishops' Bible*

English Hexapla New Testament

In 1841, the English Hexapla New Testament was printed. It served as a wonderful textual comparison tool. In parallel columns it had the following six versions of the entire New Testament:

- 1380 Wycliff
- 1534 Tyndale
- 1539 Great
- 1557 Geneva
- 1582 Rheims
- 1611 King James

Across the top of the page the original Greek was written.

The textual comparison of the New Testament's most famous verse, John 3:16, from these six Bibles is as follows.

1st Ed. *King James* (1611)

"For God so loued the world, that he gaue his only begotten Sonne: that whosoeuer beleeueth in him, should not perish, but haue euerlasting life."

Rheims (1582)

"For so God loued the vvorld, that he gaue his only-begotten sonne: that euery one that beleeueth in him, perish not, but may haue life euerlasting."

Geneva (1557)

"For God so loueth the world, that he hath geuen his only begotten Sonne: that none that beleue in him, should peryshe, but haue euerlasting lyfe."

Great Bible (1539)

"For God so loued the worlde, that he gaue his only begotten sonne, that whosoeuer beleueth in him, shulde not perisshe, but haue euerlasting lyfe."

Tyndale (1534)

"For God so loveth the worlde, that he hath geven his only sonne, that none that beleve in him, shuld perisshe: but shuld have everlastinge lyfe."

Wycliffe (1380)

"for god loued so the world; that he gaf his oon bigetun sone, that eche man that bileueth in him perisch not: but haue euerlastynge liif."

It is possible to go back to manuscripts earlier than Wycliffe, but the language is not easily recognizable. For example, the Anglo-Saxon manuscript of AD 995 renders John 3:16 as:

"God lufode middan-eard swa, dat he seade his an-cennedan sunu, dat nan ne forweorde de on hine gely ac habbe dat ece lif."

English Bible translations before 1611

Wycliffe's version

1. Everyday language

Wycliffe's version used ordinary speech.

- For the word "children" he used "brat"
- For the word "father" he used "dad"
- For the word "chariot" he used "cart"

2. A literal version

Wycliffe's version was a literal translation.

"The disciplis scein to hym, Maister now the Jewis soughten for to stoone thee, and est goist thou thidir? Jheus answered whether ther ben not twelue ouris of the dai? If ony man wandre in the night he stomblish, for light is not in him. He seith these thingis and aftir these things heseith to them Lazarus oure freend slepith but Y go to reise hym fro sleep. Therfor hise disciplis seiden: Lord if he slepith he schal be saaf."

Below: Tyndale's New Testament.

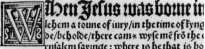

Tyndale's version

1. Everyday language

Tyndale's translation of Titus 1:1 reads, "Paul, the rascal of God and the villein of Jesus Christ."

2. Sense of the original

Tyndale tried to convey the sense of the original Hebrew and Greek words.

In place of	*Tyndale used the word*
• Grace	Favor
• Charity	Love
• Confessing	Acknowledging
• Priests	Elders
• Penance	Repentance
• Church	Congregation

Coverdale

Miles Coverdale's translation was the first full Bible to be printed in English. It is noted for the beauty of its phrasing and rhythms.

The *Matthew Bible*

Although the title page of this Bible claims to be purely the work of Thomas Matthew it was in reality an edited version of Tyndale's Bible. It was a great irony that while Tyndale's translation work and theological views caused him to be strangled and burned at the stake, praying the words, "Lord, open the King of England's eyes," with his last gasp, *Matthew's Bible* became the first "authorized" English Bible. For Thomas Cranmer, the then Archbishop of Canterbury, persuaded Henry VIII to

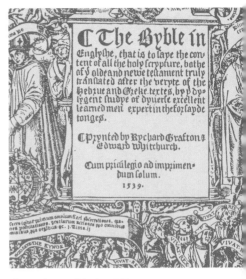

give this Bible his official sanction.

The *Great Bible*

This was Coverdale's edited version of *Matthew's Bible*. It was called the "Great Bible" because the size of its pages measured 9 in. by 15 in. It became the official Bible in England and was ordered to be displayed prominently in every church in England. The psalms from the Great Bible, popularly known as "Coverdale's psalms," are still printed in *The Book of Common Prayer*.

Above: Title page of the Great Bible.

The *Geneva Bible*

More than 200 editions of the *Geneva Bible* were published and it became the most popular English Bible between 1570 and 1620. It had a great influence on the *King James Version*. Under the leadership of William Whittingham many leading Protestant scholars who lived in Geneva worked on this translation. It also included extensive notes on the text of the Bible and so is known as the first Study Bible. It was the first Bible to be taken to America and was the Bible of the Puritans and the Pilgrim Fathers.

Bishops' Bible

Archbishop Parker promoted this revision of the *Great Bible*. It was printed in an elaborate and elegant way with ornamented capital letters and lavish illustrations. While it received ecclesiastical authorization, it was never embraced by scholars and its cost

prevented it from every becoming popular. However, the 1572 edition of its New Testament section had a significant influence on the *King James Version*.

The *Rheims* and *Douay* versions

Roman Catholics who had fled from England published a New Testament at Rheims in 1582. The Old Testament was published in Douay in 1611. Unlike the Protestant translators whose overriding aim was to produce a Bible version in the vernacular, Gregory Martin, William Allen, and the other translators paid more attention to their translation being an accurate translation of the Latin *Vulgate* than to intelligibility. Its one influence on the *King James Version* is that it broadened the word base on which it was constructed. The *Douay Bible* became the principal English Catholic Bible until the creation of the *Jerusalem Bible* in the mid-twentieth century.

The transmission of the Bible to English

INFLUENTIAL BIBLES	
500 BC	Completion of all original Hebrew manuscripts which make up the 39 Books of the Old Testament.
200 BC	Completion of the Septuagint Greek manuscripts which contain the 39 Old Testament books.
1st century AD	Completion of all original Greek Manuscripts which make up the 27 books of the New Testament.
390	Jerome's Latin *Vulgate* manuscripts produced which contain the whole Bible.
995	Anglo-Saxon (early roots of the English language) translations of the New Testament produced.
1384	Wycliffe produces the first manuscript copy of the complete Bible in English, which he wrote out by hand. Wycliffe had no access to Greek or Hebrew manuscripts and so relied on the fourth-century Latin translation of St Jerome.
1455	Gutenberg invents the printing press, so books can now be mass-produced instead of being individually hand-written. It took a scribe ten months to write out one copy of the Bible. The first book from the press was the Latin *Vulgate*, called the "Mazarin Bible," because copies of it were found in the library of Cardinal Mazarin at Paris.

1516	Erasmus produces a Greek/Latin parallel New Testament.
1522	Martin Luther translates the New Testament into German.
1526	William Tyndale produces his translation of the New Testament, the first New Testament to be printed in the English Language.
1530	Tyndale's translation of the Pentateuch (the first five books of the Old Testament) is printed.
1535	Miles Coverdale's Bible was the first complete Bible to be printed in the English language.
1537	The *Matthew Bible* is published and is the second complete Bible to be printed in English.
1539	The *Great Bible* is printed and is the first English language Bible to be authorized for public use.
1560	The *Geneva Bible* is printed and is the first English language Bible to have verse numbers and chapter divisions included in it.
1568	The *Bishops' Bible* is printed. It became one of the main sources for the *King James Bible*.
1609	The *Douay Old Testament* is added to the *Rheims New Testament* (of 1582) and so completed the first complete English Catholic Bible.

1611	The *King James Bible* is printed.
1782	The *Robert Aitken Bible* is printed and becomes the first English language Bible (a *King James Version* without Apocrypha) to be printed in America.
1791	Isaac Collins and Isaiah Thomas respectively produce the first family Bible and first illustrated Bible printed in America. Both were *King James Versions*.
1808	Jane Aitken, the daughter of Robert Aitken, produces the first Bible to be printed by a woman.
1833	Noah Webster's Bible. After producing his famous dictionary, Webster printed his own revision of the *King James Bible*.
1841	The *English Hexapla New Testament*, an early textual comparison showing the Greek and six famous English translations in parallel columns, is produced.
1885	The *Revised Version Bible*, the first major English revision of the *King James Bible*, is produced.
1901	The *American Standard Version*, the first major American revision of the *King James Bible*, is produced.

1971	The *New American Standard Bible (NASB)* is published purporting to be a "modern and accurate word for word English translation" of the Bible.
1973	The *New International Version (NIV)* is published purporting to be a "modern and accurate phrase for phrase English translation" of the Bible.
1982	The *New King James Version (NKJV)* is published purporting to be a "modern English version maintaining the original style of the *King James*."

The King James Version

The story of the *King James Version*
The Hampton Court conference
In 1604, at the Hampton Court conference, Dr. Reynolds, President of Corpus Christi College, Oxford, and spokesman for the moderate Puritans, suggested that a new translation of the Bible should be made. Unlike the *Geneva Bible* it would not have any marginal notes. James I of England wholeheartedly embraced this idea.

The need for a new translation
The *Preface* to the *Authorized King James Version* of 1611 states:

"Happy is the man that delighted in the Scripture, and thrice happy that meditateth in it day and night.

But how shall men meditate in that, which they cannot understand? How shall they understand that which is kept close in an unknown tongue?... Nature taught a natural man to confess, that all of us in those tongues which we do not understand, are plainly deaf...In the Senate of Rome, there was one or other that called for an interpreter: so lest the Church be driven to the like exigent, it is necessary to have translations in a readiness. Translation it is that openeth the window, to let in the light; that breaketh the shell, that we may eat the kernel; that putteth aside the curtain, that we may look into the most Holy place; that removeth the cover of the well, that we may come by the water, even as Jacob rolled away the stone from the mouth of the well, by which means the flocks of Laban were watered [Gen 29:10]. Indeed without translation into the vulgar tongue, the unlearned are but like children at Jacob's well (which is deep) [John 4:11] without a bucket or something to draw with; or as that person mentioned by Isaiah, to whom when a sealed book was delivered, with this motion, "Read this, I pray thee," he was fain to make this answer, "I cannot, for it is sealed." [Isa 29:11]

The Translators to the Readers
In its preface, entitled, *The Translators to the Readers*, the translators make it clear that they never intended to make a completely new translation. Nor did they intend to turn a bad translation into a good translation. Rather, they aimed "to make a good one better, or out of many good ones, one principal good one, not justly to be excepted against."

They wanted to produce a Bible that spoke for itself, and which could be understood by everyone, "euen of the very vulgar."

Leading scholars
King James appointed 54 scholars, mainly from the universities of Oxford and Cambridge. They followed Langton's chapter divisions. The leading biblical scholars of the time worked in six

Below: Title page of the King James Version, 1611.

groups, with each group translating a section of the Bible. The translation work kept the following rules:

- the *Bishops' Bible* was to serve as the basis for the new version
- the most commonly used version of proper names was to be used
- the old version of disputed words was to be used (so the word "church" was instead of "congregation")
- marginal notes would be used only to explain Greek or Hebrew words or to point to parallel passages
- existing chapter and verse divisions would be kept but new headings would be created for the chapters.

Other versions used

Unlike some modern Bible versions which do not always acknowledge their indebtedness to previous translations of the Bible, the translators of the *King James Version* were only too pleased to state which sources they used.

For the Old Testament they mainly relied on ben Hayyim's edition of the ben Asher text.

For the New Testament they used Erasmus' Greek text and the bilingual Greek-and-Latin text from the sixth century, which had been discovered by Theodore Beza.

They used the *Bishops' Bible*, which relied on the *Great Bible*, which relied on Tyndale's work, as their main English translation.

So while the *King James Version* was a completely new translation it relied heavily on: *Tyndale's New Testament*, The *Coverdale Bible*, The *Matthew Bible*, The *Great Bible*, The *Geneva Bible*. It also made occasional use of the *Rheims New Testament*. About 66% of the new translation is indebted to earlier English Bibles, with approximately 19% from the *Geneva New Testament* and 18% from the *Matthew Bible* and Tyndale's translations.

The Authorized Version

Although this Bible is commonly called the *Authorized Version*, it was never officially authorized by either church or state. But because James I had authorized the initial translation work, and because of his support for it, it became known as the *Authorized Version*. Also, the words "appointed to be read in churches" appeared in the initial edition of 1611. Few disagree that it is still the "noblest monument of English prose."

A contemporary Bible translator

"Certainly my experience of this close encounter with the text has been the same as that of J. B. Phillips a generation ago. The closer you get to it, the more it rings true. In particular, the closer you get to the words of Jesus, even though, of course, he probably spoke Aramaic, not Greek, the more they stand out as the powerful words of the most extraordinary man ever to walk the earth. And, whatever theory you hold of the Bible, I have been conscious of the power that this text possesses, and of its God-giveneess." Dr Tom Wright, Canon Theologian of Westminster Abbey

20th-century English Bible translations

EIGHT VERSIONS			
Bible version	*Date*	*Translated by*	*Features*
American Standard Version (ASV)	1901	American scholars	A revision of the *English Revised Version*, which was a revision of the *KJV*.
Revised Standard Version (RSV)	1929	An ecumenical committee	It altered the wording of some classic passages. A few pivotal passages are not translated in conservative way.
Jeruasalem Bible (JB)	1966	Roman Catholic scholars	Excellent literary style.
New American Standard Bible (NASB)	1971	American scholars	Evangelical. An update of the *ASV*. Hebrew and Greek names are transliterated.
Living Bible (LB)	1971	Kenneth N. Taylor	Paraphrase in contemporary American. Originally written to read to his children. The *New Living Translation* (1996) updated the *LB*.
Today's English Version	1976	American Bible Society	Straightforward English. Has over 500 line drawings. Used by children and people whose first language is not English.
New International Version (NIV)	1978	110 international, evangelical scholars. New York International Bible Society	Sets out to be an accurate, dignified, yet contemporary translation.
New King James Version (NKJV)	1982	130 evangelical scholars	It aimed to update the *KJV*. It replaces out of date words but retains the flowing cadences of the *KJV*.
The Message	1993	Eugene H. Peterson	Paraphrase in contemporary idiom which seeks to "convert the tone, the rhythm, the events, the ideas [of the NT], into the way we actually think and speak."

Bible versions:

THREE VERSIONS OF 1 CORINTHIANS 13 COMPARED

KING JAMES VERSION

1 Though I speak with the tongues of men and of angels, and have not charity, I am become as sounding brass, or a tinkling cymbal.

2 And though I have the gift of prophecy, and understand all mysteries, and all knowledge; and though I have all faith, so that I could remove mountains, and have not charity, I am nothing.

3 And though I bestow all my goods to feed the poor, and though I give my body to be burned, and have not charity, it profiteth me nothing.

4 Charity suffereth long, and is kind; charity envieth not; charity vaunteth not itself, is not puffed up,

5 Doth not behave itself unseemly, seeketh not her own, is not easily provoked, thinketh no evil;

6 Rejoiceth not in iniquity, but rejoiceth in the truth;

7 Beareth all things, believeth all things, hopeth all things, endureth all things.

8 Charity never faileth: but whether there be prophecies, they shall fail; whether there be tongues, they shall cease; whether there be knowledge, it shall vanish away.

9 For we know in part, and we prophesy in part.

10 But when that which is perfect is come, then that which is in part shall be done away.

11 When I was a child, I spake as a child, I understood as a child, I thought as a child: but when I became a man, I put away childish things.

12 For now we see through a glass, darkly; but then face to face: now I know in part; but then shall I know even as also I am known.

13 And now abideth faith, hope, charity, these three; but the greatest of these is charity.

NEW INTERNATIONAL VERSION

1 If I speak in tongues of men and of angels, but have not love, I am only a resounding gong or a clanging cymbal.

2 If I have the gift of prophecy and can fathom all mysteries and all knowledge, and if I have a faith that can move mountains, but have not love, I am nothing.

3 If I give all I possess to the poor and surrender my body to the flames, but have not love, I gain nothing.

4 Love is patient, love is kind. It does not envy, it does not boast, it is not proud.

5 It is not rude, it is not self-seeking, it is not easily angered, it keeps no record of wrongs.

6 Love does not delight in evil but rejoices with the truth.

7 It always protects, always trusts, always hopes, always perseveres.

8 Love never fails. But where there are prophecies, they will cease; where there are tongues, they will be stilled; where there is knowledge, it will pass away.

9 For we know in part and we prophesy in part,

10 but when perfection comes, the imperfect disappears.

11 When I was a child, I talked like a child, I thought like a child, I reasoned like a child. When I became a man, I put childish ways behind me.

12 Now we see but a poor reflection as in a mirror; then we shall see face to face. Now I know in part; then I shall know fully, even as I am fully known.

13 And now these three remain: faith, hope and love. But the greatest of these is love.

THE MESSAGE

If I speak with human eloquence and angelic ecstasy but don't love, I'm nothing but the creaking of a rusty gate.

If I speak God's Word with power, revealing all his mysteries and making everything plain as day, and if I have faith that says to a mountain "Jump," and it jumps, but I don't love, I'm nothing.

If I give everything I own to the poor and even go to the stake to be burned as a martyr, but I don't love, I've gotten nowhere. So, no matter what I say, what I believe, and what I do, I'm bankrupt without love.

Love never gives up.

Love cares more for others than for self. Love doesn't want what it doesn't have.

Love doesn't strut,

Doesn't have a swelled head,

Doesn't force itself on others,

Isn't always "me first,"

Doesn't fly off the handle,

Doesn't keep score of the sins of others,

Doesn't revel when others grovel,

Take pleasure in the flowering of truth,

Puts up with anything,

Trusts God always,

Always looks for the best,

Never looks back,

But keeps going to the end.

Love never dies. Inspired speech will be over some day: praying in tongues will end; understanding will reach its limit. We know only a portion of the truth, and what we say about God is always incomplete. But when the Complete arrives, our incompletes will be canceled.

When I was an infant at my mother's breast, I gurgled and cooed like any infant. When I grew up, I left those infant ways for good.

We don't yet see things clearly. We're squinting in a fog, peering through a mist. But it won't be long before the weather clears and the sun shines bright! We'll see it all then, see it all as clearly as God sees us, knowing him directly just as he knows us!

But for right now, until that completeness, we have three things to do to lead us toward that consummation: Trust steadily in God, hope unswervingly, love extravagantly. And the best of the three is love.

Evaluating Bible versions

1. Is it a revision of the *King James Version*?

There are a number of Bibles which attempt to update the *King James Version*, such as:

- The *English Revised Version*
- The *American Standard Version*
- The *Revised Standard Version*
- The *New American Standard Version*
- The *New King James Version*

2. Does it have any denominational bias?

Most recently produced Bibles attempt to have no denominational bias, but some Bible versions have been translated by scholars drawn from one particular denomination, such as the *Jerusalem Bible* and the *New American Bible* which were produced by Roman Catholic scholars.

3. Is it a paraphrase or a translation?

Some Bible versions, such as J. B. Philipps' *New Testament in Modern English*, deliberately set out to be paraphrases. They attempt to convey the basic meaning of each Hebrew or Greek phrase, even if this means that they do not keep rigidly to a word-for-word translation.

4. Does the version use the dynamic equivalent?

Today's English Version (*Good News for Modern Man*) uses the dynamic equivalent in its translation. Eugene Nida rejected the traditional means of translation, often referred to as formal equivalence, which concentrates on the need to preserve all the features possible from the original language. The dynamic equivalent translator aims not only to express what the original author said, but also what he meant to say. The *AV*, *ASV* and the *NASV* follow this principle of translation. Nida, rather than concentrating on transferring the meaning of individual words, focuses on the underlying structure or kernel in the source language, and then transfers the meaning of this unit from one language to another.

Nida explained this from Mark 1:4, which literalistically can be translated, "John preached a baptism of repentance for the forgiveness of sins." Nida felt that phrases such as "baptism of repentance" and "forgiveness of sins" mean little to today's readers. So the sense of the sentence is conveyed more meaningfully in the following way, "John preached, 'Repent and be baptized, so that God will forgive the evil you have done.'"

Some linguists maintain that children find Bibles which employ the dynamic equivalent principle the most easy to understand.

5. Seek out its theological viewpoint

Often the preface to a Bible will give you the theological stance of the translator or translators. The preface of the *New International Version* states that its translators are "united in their commitment to the authority and infallibility of the Bible as God's Word in

Below: Latin Bible, 1608.

written form." So it would be safe to conclude that this translation comes from the pens of conservative evangelicals.

6. Inclusive language

Some Bibles have been written in what is called "gender-free," or, inclusive language. While the *Jerusalem Bible* attempted to address this issue in a small way the *New Revised Standard Version* and the *Revised English Bible* were the first major Bibles published which incorporated inclusive language in their translations.

An inclusive language edition of the *New International Version* was published in England in 1995 and hardly caused any stir. It was welcomed with open arms by some. John Stott wrote of it, "I welcome this inclusive language edition of the New Testament, Psalms and

Proverbs...There has been no meddlesome tampering with language which relates to God; only what relates to us has been changed. And these modifications are essential. When "man" means human being, without any intention to exclude women, and when the use of "brothers" was never intended to exclude sisters, then to retain such gender-specific words would be offensive. Even worse, it would actually misrepresent the meaning of the biblical text."

But an inclusive edition of the *NIV* published in the United States caused so much controversy that the publishes withdrew it.

In an inclusive Bible the disciples are no longer told that they will be "fishers of men" but are told by Jesus, "I will make you fish for people" (Matthew 4:19 *NRSV*).

3 | *FASCINATING FEATURES ABOUT INDIVIDUAL OLD TESTAMENT BOOKS*

CONTENTS

Introduction

There are many ways of studying individual Old Testament books. Here we select just one different topic in each Bible book and see how it is treated. So in the book of Job, the advice given to suffering Job by his so-called comforters, Elphaz, Bildad, Zophar and Elihu, is examined. In the case of another book, a significant person is at the heart of the study, as in the book of Judges, where Samson is put under the microscope. The fulfilment of prophecy is the theme tackled in the study from the book of Isaiah, where 17 of its prophecies are found to be fulfilled in the life of Christ.

These 36 studies show that profitable spiritual lessons may be found in every Old Testament book.

Genesis

TEN TYPES OF JESUS

"TYPES"		
A "type" is a historical fact which illustrates a spiritual truth. In the book of Genesis, as throughout the Old Testament, there are people who are types of Jesus, and there are events which serve as types of Jesus.		
Types of Jesus in Genesis	*Reason for being a type of Jesus*	*Bible verses*
1. Adam	Adam is the head of the old creation. Jesus is the head of the new creation.	"…Adam, who was a type of the one to come" Romans 5:14.
2. Adam and Eve	Adam and Eve are types of Christ and his church.	Compare Genesis 2:23, 24 with Ephesians 5:31, 32: "'For this reason a man will leave his father and mother and be united to his wife, and the two will become one flesh.' This is a profound mystery–but I am talking about Christ and his church."
3. Tree of life	According to John 1:4 spiritual life is in Jesus.	"In the middle of the garden were the tree of life and the tree of knowledge of good and evil" Genesis 2:9. "To him who overcomes, I will give the right to eat from the tree of life, which is the paradise of God" Revelation 2:7.
4. Abel	Abel's sacrifice of a blood sacrifice points to Jesus' death on the cross.	Compare Genesis 4:4 with Hebrews 11:4: "By faith Abel offered God a better sacrifice than Cain did. By faith he was commended as a righteous man, when God spoke well of his offerings."
5. Noah	By obeying God in building the ark Noah prepared the way of salvation for his family and the animals.	Compare Genesis 6:14 with Hebrews 11:7: "By faith Noah when warned about things not yet seen, in holy fear built an ark to save his family. By his faith he condemned the world and became heir of the righteousness that comes by faith."

6. Melchizedek	Melchizedek, the righteous king, and priest-king, is likened to Jesus.	Compare Genesis 14:18-20 with Hebrews 7:1, 3: "This Melchizedek was king of Salem and priest of God Most High...Without father or mother, without genealogy, without beginning of days or end of life, like the Son of God he remains a priest for ever."
7. Abraham	Abraham was head of many nations, Jesus is the spiritual head of all nations.	Compare Genesis 17:5 with Galatians 3:8: "The Scripture foresaw that God would justify the Gentiles by faith, and announced the gospel in advance to Abraham: 'All nations will be blessed through you.'"
8. Isaac	Isaac, Abraham's one and only son, was offered as a sacrifice. He also prefigures Jesus' resurrection.	Compare Genesis 22:1-14 with Hebrews 11:17-19: "By faith Abraham, when God tested him, offered Isaac as a sacrifice. He who had received the promises was about to sacrifice his one and only son, even though God had said to him, 'It is through Isaac that your offspring will be reckoned.' Abraham reasoned that God could raise the dead, and figuratively speaking, he did receive Isaac back from death."
9. Ram caught in a thicket	God provided a ram for Abraham and Jesus as the sacrificial substitute for sin.	"Abraham looked up and there in a thicket he saw a ram caught by its horns" Genesis 22:13.

"Therefore, when Christ came into the world, he said: "Sacrifice and offering you did not desire, but a body you prepared for me; with burnt offerings and sin offerings you were not pleased. Then I said, 'Here I am–it is written about me in the scroll–I have come to do your will, O God.' First he said, 'Sacrifices and offerings, burnt offerings and sin offerings you did not desire, nor were you pleased with them' (although the law required them to be made). Then he said, 'Here I am, I have come to do your will.' He sets aside the first to establish the second. And by that will, we have been made holy through the sacrifice of the body of Jesus Christ once for all." Hebrews 10:5-10

10. Joseph	Both Joseph and Jesus were especially loved by their fathers, hated by their families, rejected as rulers over their families, sold for silver and condemned though innocent.	Compare Genesis 37:3 with Matthew 3:17; John 3:35; Genesis 37:4, 5, 8 with John 15:25; Genesis 37:28 with Matthew 26:15; Genesis 39:16-18 with Matthew 26:59, 60.

Exodus

SIX THINGS IN EXODUS EXPLAINED BY HEBREWS

HEBREWS		
The book of Hebrews explains the theological significance of the sacrificial system which God instituted in the book of Exodus.		
Topic	*Exodus reference*	*Hebrews reference*
1. A pattern. The method of worship in Exodus is a pattern to follow	25:40	8:3-5 Every high priest is appointed to offer both gifts and sacrifices, and so it was necessary for this one also to have something to offer. If he were on earth, he would not be a priest, for there are already men who offer the gifts prescribed by the law. They serve at a sanctuary that is a copy and shadow of what is in heaven. This is why Moses was warned when he was about to build the tabernacle: "See to it that you make everything according to the pattern shown you on the mountain."
2. The bodies of sacrificed animals burned	29:14	13:11-14 The high priest carries the blood of animals into the Most Holy Place as a sin offering, but the bodies are burned outside the camp. And so Jesus also suffered outside the city gate to make the people holy through his own blood. Let us, then, go to him outside the camp, bearing the disgrace he bore. For here we do not have an enduring city, but we are looking for the city that is to come.
3. The blood of the covenant	24:6 Moses took the blood, sprinkled it on the people and said, "This is the blood of the covenant that the Lord has made with you in accordance with all these words."	9:19-22 When Moses had proclaimed every commandment of the law to all the people, he took the blood of calves, together with water, scarlet wool and branches of hyssop, and sprinkled the scroll and all the people. He said, "This is the blood of the covenant, which God has commanded you to keep." In the same way, he sprinkled with the blood both the tabernacle and everything used in its ceremonies. In fact, the law requires that nearly everything be cleansed with blood, and without the shedding of blood there is no forgiveness.

4. The tabernacle and its furniture	25:26; 40	9:1-6 Now the first covenant had regulations for worship and also an earthly sanctuary. A tabernacle was set up. In its first room were the lampstand, the table and the consecrated bread; this was called the Holy Place. Behind the second curtain was a room called the Most Holy Place, which had the golden altar of incense and the gold-covered ark of the covenant. This ark contained the gold jar of manna, Aaron's staff that had budded, and the stone tablets of the covenant. Above the ark were the cherubim of the Glory, overshadowing the atonement cover. But we cannot discuss these things in detail now. When everything had been arranged like this, the priests entered regularly into the outer room to carry on their ministry.
5. The day of atonement	30:10	9:7 But only the high priest entered the inner room, and that only once a year, and never without blood, which he offered for himself and for the sins the people had committed in ignorance.
6. Mount Sinai	19:12, 19	12:18-22 You have not come to a mountain that can be touched and that is burning with fire; to darkness, gloom and storm; to a trumpet blast or to such a voice speaking words that those who heard it begged that no further word be spoken to them, because they could not bear what was commanded: "If even an animal touches the mountain, it must be stoned." The sight was so terrifying that Moses said, "I am trembling with fear." But you have come to Mount Zion, to the heavenly Jerusalem, the city of the living God.

Leviticus

SEVEN FEASTS IN LEVITICUS

THE SEVEN FEASTS		
In Leviticus chapter 23 seven feasts are mentioned which are all elaborated on in the New Testament.		
Name of feast	*Commemorates*	*New Testament link*
The Passover Leviticus 23:4-5	This commemorated Israel's deliverance from Egypt	Jesus is our Passover Lamb by whose substitutionary death our forgiveness is possible. "For Christ, our Passover Lamb, has been sacrificed" 1 Corinthians 5:7.
Unleavened Bread Leviticus 23:6-8	This feast also commemorated Israel's escape from Egypt	Unleavened bread speaks of the holiness required of believers. "For you know what instructions we gave you by the authority of the Lord Jesus. It is God's will that you should be sanctified: that you should avoid sexual immorality; that each of you should learn to control his own body in a way that is holy and honorable, not in passionate lust like the heathen, who do not know God; and that in this matter no one should wrong his brother or take advantage of him. The Lord will punish men for all such sins, as we have already told you and warned you. For God did not call us to be impure, but to live a holy life" 1 Thessalonians 4:3-7.
Firstfruits Leviticus 23:9-14	This feast commemorated the harvest	This feast speaks of Jesus' resurrection as the firstfruit of the resurrection of all Christians. "But Christ has indeed been raised from the dead, the firstfruits of those who have fallen asleep" 1 Corinthians 15:20.

Pentecost/Feast of Weeks Leviticus 23:15-22	Pentecost celebrated harvest	Pentecost speaks of the coming of the Holy Spirit after Jesus' ascension. "When the day of Pentecost came, they were all together in one place. Suddenly a sound like the blowing of a violent wind came from heaven and filled the whole house where they were sitting. They saw what seemed to be tongues of fire that separated and came to rest on each of them. All of them were filled with the Holy Spirit and began to speak in other tongues as the Spirit enabled them" Acts 2:1-4.
Trumpets Leviticus 23:23-25	This was the beginning of the civil year, corresponding to our New Year's Day	"For the Lord himself will come down from heaven, with a loud command, with the voice of the archangel and with the trumpet call of God, and the dead in Christ will rise first" 1 Thessalonians 4:16.
Day of Atonement Leviticus 23:26-32	The Day of Atonement commemorated the day when atonement was made for the sins of the nation of Israel	Jesus atoned for our sins when he died on the cross. "For this reason he had to be made like his brothers in every way, in order that he might become a merciful and faithful high priest in service to God, and that he might make atonement for the sins of the people" Hebrews 2:17.
Tabernacles Leviticus 23:33-43	The feast of Tabernacles, or Booths, commemorated Israel's life and wanderings in the desert	Jesus is our Redeemer. "For he has rescued us from the dominion of darkness and brought us into the kingdom of the Son he loves, in whom we have redemption, the forgiveness of sins" Colossians 1:13, 14.

Key words in the book of Leviticus

Atonement

This refers to a covering of sin which makes possible a relationship with God.

Clean

If a person was ritually and morally pure he could participate in the community's worship of God.

Guilt

When anyone committed a sin God declared him guilty.

Sacrifice

Sacrifices were ritual offerings of the blood of animals. The slaughtered animal took the penalty for the sin of the offerer of the sacrifice.

Numbers

FIVE DIFFERENCES BETWEEN THE TEN SPIES AND JOSHUA AND CALEB

A DIFFERENT SPIRIT	
"...my servant Caleb has a different spirit and follows me wholeheartedly..." 14:24. While the ten spies doubted God, Joshua and Caleb believed in God.	
The ten spies	**Joshua and Caleb**
1. We can't attack those people: 13:31.	1. We should go up: 13:30.
2. They are stronger than we are: 13:31.	2. Their protection is gone: 14:9.
3. They spread...a bad report: 13:32.	3. The land...is exceedingly good: 14:7.
4. The land we explored devours those living in it: 13:32.	4. We will swallow them up: 14:9.
5. We seemed like grasshoppers: 13:33.	5. The Lord is with us. Do not be afraid of them. 14:9.

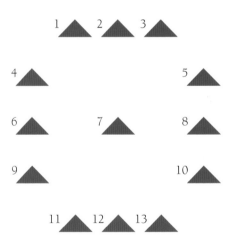

Encampment of the Tribes of Israel: Numbers 2:1-31

1 Naphtali
2 Asher
3 Dan
4 Ephraim
5 Judah
6 Manasseh
7 T A B E R N A C L E
8 Issachar
9 Benjamin
10 Zebulun
11 Gad
12 Simeon
13 Reuben

THE ORDER IN WHICH THE TRIBES OF ISRAEL MARCHED: NUMBERS 10:11-33						
Dan	Ephraim	*Kohathites carry the tabernacle furnishings*	Reuben	*Gershonites and Merarites carry the tabernacle*	Judah	*Levites carry the ark*
Asher	Manasseh		Simeon		Issachar	
Naphtali	Benjamin		Gad		Zebulun	

The bronze snake

The bronze snake is the only shadow of the cross in the Old Testament which Jesus alluded to in such a detailed and specific way.

The bronze snake in Numbers

"And the people spake against God, and against Moses, Wherefore have ye brought us up out of Egypt to die in the wilderness? for there is no bread, neither is there any water; and our soul loatheth this light bread.

And the LORD sent fiery serpents among the people, and they bit the people; and much people of Israel died.

Therefore the people came to Moses, and said, We have sinned, for we have spoken against the LORD, and against thee; pray unto the LORD, that he take away the serpents from us. And Moses prayed for the people.

And the LORD said unto Moses, Make thee a fiery serpent, and set it upon a pole: and it shall come to pass, that every one that is bitten, when he looketh upon it, shall live.

And Moses made a serpent of brass, and put it upon a pole, and it came to pass, that if a serpent had bitten any man, when he beheld the serpent of brass, he lived." *Numbers 21: 5-9 KJV*

THE BRONZE SNAKE IN JOHN		
"And as Moses lifted up the serpent in the wilderness, even so must the Son of man be lifted up:" John 3:14		
Lesson from the bronze snake	*Verse in Numbers 21*	*New Testament verse*
1. The need for salvation	6	Romans 3:23; 6:23
2. The method of salvation	8	Galatians 4:3-4
3. The condition for salvation	8	John 12:32
4. They were told to "look"	8	Isaiah 45:22
5. The extent of salvation (any man)	8	John 3:16
6. The instant effect of salvation	9	John 5:24; 2 Corinthians 5:17

Deuteronomy

FIVE PARTS OF RENEWING THE COVENANT

Five parts of a treaty

In Moses' time in Near Eastern treaties they used the same five elements as are used in the book of Deuteronomy. In the book of Deuteronomy God's covenant with his people is renewed.

1. The preamble

This takes the form of a list of the parties making the treaty. The covenant is between "the Lord" and "all Israel" (Deuteronomy 1:1-5).

2. The historical prologue

This records the kind dealings of the king in the past. See 1:6–4:43 which acts as an historical prologue to the whole book.

3. The conditions of the covenant

What God requires in his covenant is set out in great detail in 4:44–26:19

Part one is the stipulation for absolute allegiance and includes Israel's basic moral code, the Ten Commandments (4:44–11:32).

Part two has four supplementary requirements:

  a. About ceremonial consecration: 12:1–16:17
  b. About how rulers should lead a righteous nation: 16:18–21:21
  c. About how God's kingdom must be kept holy: 21:22–25:19
  d. About confessing sin to God, who is the Redeemer-King: chapter 26

4. The ratification of the covenant

These take the form of promised blessings and cursings in chapters 27–30. God's blessings come as a result of obeying him, but he curses his people when they disobey him.

5. The provisions for maintaining the covenant

This covenant is to extend into the future, chapters 31–34. It will continue even though there will be a change of leadership, as Moses dies and is succeeded by Joshua, chapter 34.

Joshua
FIVE MIRACLES

NINE CONTRASTS BETWEEN THE BOOK OF JOSHUA AND THE BOOK OF JUDGES	
The book of Joshua	*The book of Judges*
1. Faith	Unbelief
2. Victory	Defeat
3. Sin is judged	Sin is lightly regarded
4. Freedom	Defeat
5. Sense of unity	Anarchy
6. Spiritual vision	Focus on earthly things
7. Strength	Weakness
8. Joy	Sorrow
9. Faithfulness to God	Apostasy

Five miracles recorded in the book of Joshua

1. The River Jordan divides: 3:14-17
2. An angel appears to Joshua: 5:13-15
3. Jericho's walls collapse: 6:1-20
4. A storm of hailstones: 10:11
5. The sun stood still and the moon stopped: 10:11-14

Joshua in the New Testament

1. God's presence is promised: 1:5, with Hebrews 13:5
2. Rahab: 2:1-16, with James 2:25; Matthew 1:5
3. Rahab's rescue: 6:23, with Hebrews 11:31
4. Crossing the River Jordan with the ark and the tabernacle: 3:13-17, with Acts 7:44, 45
5. The fall of Jericho: 6:20, with Hebrews 11:30
6. Joseph's burial: 24:32, with Hebrews 11:22. See Genesis 50:24, 25

Judges

SIX CONTRASTING FEATURES IN SAMSON'S LIFE

1. Samson took a Nazarite vow: 13:5.
2. Samson went after an evil companion: 14:1-4.
3. Samson was at times stirred by the Spirit of the Lord: 13:25.
4. Samson was at times filled with lust: 16:1-4.
5. Samson was physically strong: 14:5, 6; 15:14, 15; 16:3, 9, 17.
6. Samson was weak in times of temptation: 16:15-17.

Ruth

SIX THINGS ABOUT A "KINSMAN-REDEEMER" AND JESUS AS REDEEMER

Kinsman-redeemer in Ruth

The book of Ruth shows how Boaz became her kinsman-redeemer. This has been taken as a "type" of Jesus, illustrating how Jesus is our Kinsman-redeemer.

1. A kinsman-redeemer must be blood related.
2. A kinsman-redeemer must be able to pay the money needed to redeem the person.
3. A kinsman-redeemer must be willing to redeem the person.
4. A kinsman-redeemer must redeem the property: Leviticus 25:25-28.
5. A kinsman-redeemer must be able to redeem the person from slavery: Leviticus 25:47-49.
6. A kinsman-redeemer must protect the needs of the extended family, Deuteronomy 25:5-10.

Boaz fulfilled all these characteristics and so could become Ruth's kinsman-redeemer.

Boaz was a relative of Mahlon, Ruth's former husband, who had died. We are not told how he was related to Mahlon, but it becomes clear that Boaz is the closest male relative Ruth had.

Jesus as Redeemer

Jesus is viewed as kinsman-redeemer for Christians in the following ways:

1. Jesus is related by blood to those he redeems: John 1:14; Romans 1:3; Philippians 2:5-8; Hebrews 2:14, 15.
2. Jesus is able to pay the price of redemption: with 2:1, compare 1 Peter 1:18, 19.
3. Jesus is willing to redeem: with 3:11, compare Matthew 20:28; John 10:15, 18; Hebrews 10:7.

1 & 2 Samuel

THREE LESSONS TO LEARN FROM THE CRIPPLE MEPHIBOSHETH

Types

David and Mephibosheth have been seen as types of a Christian's experience. David and Mephibosheth are a type of salvation which God gives through his grace. The story of David and Mephibosheth comes in 2 Samuel 9.

1. Compare Mephibosheth's condition with that of the need of a sinner:
   a. Mephibosheth was afraid and hid from the king: 9:1-3
   b. Mephibosheth was in need of help, as he was a cripple: 9:3
2. Compare David's kindness with God's love: "David asked, 'Is there anyone still left of the house of Saul to whom I can show kindness for Jonathan's sake?'" 9:1
   a. David showed his kindness: 9:1
   b. David showed his graciousness, in seeking out the undeserving: 9:1, 3
   c. David showed his generosity: 9:13

3. Compare Mephibosheth's trust in David with a Christian accepting salvation:
   a. Mephibosheth went to David: 9:6
   b. Mephibosheth showed his humility:
      He bowed down to show David honor, 9:6
      He called himself a "dead dog," 9:8
   c. Mephibosheth found himself accepted by David: 9:7
   d. Mephibosheth was welcomed into David's family circle (adopted): 9:11

Grace and gift

God's grace and the gift of salvation is set out in the following verses:

- Ephesians 2:8, 9
- Psalm 40:2
- John 1:12
- Ephesians 1:3

1 & 2 Kings

32 MIRACLES

Clusters

1 and 2 Kings record 32 unusual events and miracles.

In the Old Testament miracles often appear in clusters. The miracles associated with Elijah and Elisha are two such clusters of miraculous happenings.

1 Kings

1. Solomon's strange dream. Solomon asks for wisdom: 1 Kings 3:5-15.
2. Jeroboam's hand shrivelled, and later restored: 13:4-13.
3. A drought sent by God: 17:1.
4. Elijah is fed by ravens: 17:2-6.
5. A widow's oil and flour do not run out as she feeds Elijah: 17:10-16.
6. The bringing back to life of the son of the widow of Zarephath: 17:17-24.
7. Fire from the Lord burns up a sacrifice: 18:38.
8. The Lord sends rain to end the drought: 18:41-45.
9. Elijah is fed by an angel: 19:1-8.
10. 27,000 Syrian troops killed by a collapsing wall: 20:28-30.

2 Kings

1. Ahaziah's men are consumed by fire: 2 Kings 1:9-12.
2. The River Jordan divides for Elijah and Elisha: 2:8, 14.
3. Elijah is taken up into heaven by a chariot of fire: 2:11.
4. The waters of Jericho are made fit to drink: 2:19-22.

5. 42 mocking youths are mauled by two bears: 2:24
6. Water is provided for a large army: 3:16-20.
7. Moabites mistake the reflection of a sunrise for blood in a river: 3:21-24.
8. A widow's oil is increased so much that she can pay her debts: 4:1-7.
9. The Shunammite woman has a son: 4:14-17.
10. The widow's son is brought back to life: 4:32-36.
11. Poisonous stew is cured: 4:39-41.
12. 20 barley loaves feed 100 men: 4:42-4.
13. Naaman is healed of his leprosy: 5:10-14.
14. Gehazi is made to have leprosy: 5:24-27.
15. An ax-head floats: 6:6.
16. Elisha's servant is given a vision of the Lord's army: 6:13-17.
17. Syrians are blinded: 6:18-20.
18. A dead man comes to life after coming into contact with Elisha's bones: 13:20-21.
19. 185,000 Assyrians are found dead: 19:35, 36.
20. Hezekiah is healed: 20:1-5, 7.
21. The Lord gives Hezekiah an extra 15 years to live: 20:6, 7.
22. The sun goes backwards: 20:8-11.

1 & 2 Chronicles

12 LESSONS TO LEARN FROM BATTLING JEHOSHAPHAT

LINKING 1 CHRONICLES WITH THE NEW TESTAMENT		
Topic	*1 Chronicles*	*New Testament*
1. Jesus' genealogy	"Tamar, Judah's daughter-in-law, bore him Perez and Zerah. Judah had five sons in all. The sons of Perez: Hezron and Hamul..." 2:4, 5.	"Judah the father of Perez and Zerah, whose mother was Tamar, Perez the father of Hezron, Hezron the father of Ram" Matthew 1:3.
2. David's throne	"I will set him [David] over my house and my kingdom for ever; his throne will be established for ever" 17:14.	"The Lord will give him the throne of his father David, and he will reign over the house of Jacob for ever; his kingdom will never end" Luke 1:32, 33.
3. The Aaronic priesthood	"Aaron was set apart, he and his descendants for ever, to consecrate the most holy things, to offer sacrifices before the Lord, to minister before him and to pronounce blessings in his name for ever" 23:13.	"No one takes this honor upon himself; he must be called by God, just as Aaron was" Hebrews 5:4.

Spiritual lessons

2 Chronicles 20:1-30 records how Jehoshaphat defeated Moab and Ammon and provides many spiritual lessons for Christians to draw on. Perhaps the overall lesson is that the battle is the Lord's.

1. Jehoshaphat was frightened by the enemy: 1-3.
2. Jehoshaphat turned to the Lord for help: 3.
3. Jehoshaphat proclaimed a fast: 3
4. Jehoshaphat led God's people in prayer: 4-12.
5. Jehoshaphat openly admitted his weakness: 12.
6. Jehoshaphat was encouraged by God: 14, 15.
7. Jehoshaphat was told that the battle is God's: 15.
8. Jehoshaphat was told to stand firm: 17.
9. Jehoshaphat worshiped before the Lord: 18.
10. Jehoshaphat praised the Lord: 19-21.
11. Jehoshaphat told people to have faith in the Lord: 20.
12. Jehoshaphat thanked God in the Valley of Beracah for the victory he gave: 26-29.

Ezra

EIGHT LESSONS TO LEARN FROM EZRA

Under Artaxerxes I Ezra became Secretary of State for Jewish affairs. Ezra must have been familiar with the very impressive court of Artaxerxes. The book of Ezra reveals eight characteristics which are a perennial lesson to all God's faithful followers.

1. Ezra could be trusted: 7:11-28.
2. Ezra was a man of prayer: 8:21; 10:1.
3. Ezra displayed a daring trust in God: 8:21-23.
4. Ezra practiced self-denial: 10:6.
5. Ezra was a great reformer: 10:2-5.
6. Ezra was devoted to studying the Scripture: 7:10.
7. Ezra was a faithful expositor of the Scripture: 7:10.
8. Ezra was humble enough to show solidarity with his people's sin: 9:6-15.

Nehemiah

12 LESSONS FROM THE IDEAL WORKER FOR GOD

Nehemiah is seen in the book of Nehemiah as the ideal worker for God. He believed that prayer and hard work should go hand in hand.

1. Nehemiah prayed

a. He prayed when he heard about the state of Jerusalem: 1:4-11.
b. He fasted at the same time: 1:4.
c. He "mourned" for the state of Jerusalem: 1:4.
d. He prayed before he approached King Artaxerxes: 2:4.
e. When faced with opposition, he prayed: 4:4, 9.
f. When people made false accusations against him, he prayed: 6:8, 9.

g. When the work was completed, he prayed: 13:14.

2. Nehemiah worked

a. He worked out what needed to be done before he started: 2:11-16.
b. He organized other people in their work: 3:1-32.
c. He was an inspiration to other people in their work: 2:17, 18; 4:6, 23.
d. He arranged for the city to be defended as people worked: 4:15-18.
e. He realized how important God's work was. He called it, "a great project," 6:3.

Esther

LOOKING AT ITS 17 DUPLICATIONS

Pairs

The writer of the book of Esther loved to record things in pairs.

1. There are three groups of banquets which come in pairs.
2. The king's servants are listed twice: 1:10, 14.
3. Esther's hidden identity is reported twice: 2:10, 20.
4. There are two gatherings of women: 2:8, 19.
5. The women have two houses: 2:12-14.
6. There are two fasts: 4:3, 16.
7. Haman consults with his wife and friends twice: 5:14; 6:13.
8. Esther appears uninvited before the king twice: 5:2; 8:3.
9. Mordecai has two investitures: 6:7-11; 8:15.
10. Haman's face/head is covered twice: 6:12; 7:8.
11. Haman's sons are mentioned twice: 5:11; 9:6-10, 13, 14.
12. Harbona appears twice: 1:10; 7:9.
13. Two royal edicts: 3:12-14; 8:1-13.
14. The end of the king's anger is mentioned twice: 2:1; 7:10.
15. The Persian laws are twice said to be irrevocable: 1:19; 8:8.
16. The Jews are allowed two days in which to take vengeance: 9:5-15.
17. The commemoration of Purim is instituted with two letters: 9:20-32.

Job

ELIPHAZ, BILDAD, ZOPHAR AND ELIHU COMPARED

THE FOUR "COMFORTERS"		
Job's three friends do not offer much comfort but Elihu has good advice.		
Comforter	Argument	Key verse/s
Eliphaz	Only the wicked suffer	4:8; 5:17 "As I have observed, those who plough evil and those who sow trouble reap it"
Bildad	The wicked always perish	8:13 "Such is the destiny of all who forget God; so perishes the hope of the godless"
Zophar	The wicked have short lives	20:5 "...the mirth of the wicked is brief, the joy of the godless lasts but a moment"
Elihu	Humble yourself before God	37:23 "The Almighty is beyond our reach and exalted in power;... therefore men revere him"

Psalms

TOPICAL GUIDE TO THE PSALMS

Five categories

There are many different ways of categorizing the Psalms. The following one suggests five categories. There are many other categories and many psalms fit into more than a single category.

1. Psalms about the king 2; 18; 20; 21; 45; 72; 89; 110; 132

2. Psalms about living in a godly way 1; 15; 19; 26; 36; 37; 49; 50; 52; 82; 101; 112; 119; 125; 127; 128

3. Psalms about testifying to God's goodness 9; 16; 23; 27; 30; 32; 34; 40; 41; 46; 63; 66; 78; 84; 91; 92; 103; 106; 107; 116; 118; 121; 124; 126; 131; 138; 139; 144

4. Psalms of praise 8; 24; 29; 33; 46; 47; 48; 65; 67; 68; 75; 76; 81; 87; 93; 95; 96; 97; 98; 99; 100; 104; 105; 108; 111; 113; 114; 115; 117; 122; 133; 134; 135; 136; 145; 146; 147; 148; 149; 150

5. Psalms for times of trouble 3; 4; 5; 6; 7; 10; 11; 12; 13; 14; 17; 22; 25; 28; 31; 35; 38; 39; 42; 43; 44; 51; 54; 55; 56; 57; 58; 59; 60; 61; 62; 64; 69; 71; 73; 74; 77; 79; 80; 83; 85; 86; 88; 90; 94; 102; 109; 120; 123; 129; 130; 137; 140; 141; 142; 143

Ten categories

Another way of dividing up the psalms for the purpose of study is to see which of the following ten categories they fall into.

1. Prayers for the individual 3:7-8

2. An individual praising God for his help 30; 34

3. Prayers of the community 12; 44; 79

4. The community praising God for his help 66; 75

5. Confidence in God being expressed 11; 16; 52

6. Hymns in praise of God's majesty and other virtues 8; 19; 29; 65

7. Hymns in praise of God's rule throughout the world 47; 93-97

8. Psalms about God's city, Zion 46; 48; 76; 84; 122; 126; 137

9. Teaching psalms 1; 34; 37; 73; 112; 128; 119

10. Psalms about the Lord's anointed, known as "royal" psalms 2; 18; 20; 45; 72; 89; 110

Proverbs
TOPICAL GUIDE TO PROVERBS

Adultery 5:1-6; 6:24-32; 7:6-27

"For the lips of an adulteress drip honey, and her speech is smoother than oil; but in the end she is bitter as gall, sharp as a double-edged sword" 5:3-4.

Discipline 9:7-10; 23:13, 14; 29:15, 17

Drinking 23:20, 21, 29-35; 31:4-7
"Do not join those who drink too much wine" 23:20.

Envy 3:31, 32; 6:34, 35; 24:1, 2, 19, 20

Family life 1:8, 9; 4:1-4; 6:20-33; 17:6, 21, 25; 19:13, 18, 26; 20:7, 11, 20; 23:13, 14, 22, 24

Foolish people 12:15, 16, 23; 14:3, 7-9; 17:12, 16, 28

Friendship 1:10-19; 17:17; 18:1, 24; 27:6, 10

"A friend loves at all times, and a brother is born for adversity" 17:17.

Giving 11:24, 25; 22:9, 16; 28:25, 27

God, The Lord 3:5-8, 11, 12, 25, 26; 5:20, 21; 9:10-12; 10:3, 22, 27, 29; 14:2, 16, 26, 27, 31; 15:3, 8, 9, 33; 16:2-5, 7, 9, 20, 33; 19:3,17, 18, 23; 22:2, 12, 23; 24:21, 22; 25:2, 21, 22; 28:14, 25; 30:5-9

Good deeds 3:27, 28; 14:19, 22; 25:21, 22

"Do not withhold good from those who deserve it, when it is in your power to act" 3:27.

Gossip 11:13; 16:28; 18:8; 20:19

"A gossip betrays a confidence; so avoid a man who talks too much" 20:19.

Laziness 6:9-11; 12:24, 27; 24:30-34; 26:13-16

"Diligent hands will rule, but laziness ends in slave labor" 12:24.

Love 17:9, 17; 19:22; 20:6

Lying 6:16, 17; 12:17-19, 22; 14:5, 24; 17:4, 20; 24:28, 29; 25:9, 10, 18; 26:24-28

"The Lord detests lying lips, but he delights in men who are truthful" 12:22

Poverty and wealth 6:10, 11; 10:4, 15; 11:4, 28; 13:8, 18, 23; 14:20, 31; 19:1, 4, 7, 17, 22; 22:2, 7, 9, 16, 22, 23; 23:4-8; 24:30-34; 28:8, 20, 25

Prayer 15:29; 28:9

Pride 6:16, 17; 16:5, 18; 25:6, 7; 29:1, 23

Reverence of God 1:7; 3:7, 9; 14:26, 27; 15:16, 33

Speaking 10:11, 18, 21, 31, 32; 13:2, 3; 15:1, 2, 4, 7

Wealth *see* Poverty and wealth

Wicked people 1:10-19; 2:12-15, 22: 3:33-35; 4:14-19; 10:3, 6, 16, 24, 25, 28, 30; 11:3, 5-7, 10, 18, 21, 23, 31; 28:1, 11, 12

Wisdom 1:2-7; 2:1-22; 3:1-4, 13-18; 4:7-9; 8:1-36; 9:10-12; 24:5, 14

Women 27:15, 16; 31:10-31

Ecclesiastes

SEVEN MEANINGLESS WAYS OF LIVING TRANSFORMED

Like many contemporary philosophers the Preacher illustrates how life lived according to the godless values of the world is ultimately dissatisfying and meaningless. The New Testament frequently teaches how Jesus gives the profoundest fulfilment to our earthly lives.

Life lived according to worldly attitudes

1. What is the point of work? "What does man gain from all his labor at which he toils under the sun?" *Ecclesiastes 1:3*

2. "...there is nothing new under the sun." *1:9*

3. "All the deeds done under the sun... are meaningless." *1:14*

4. "I hated all the things I toiled for under the sun." *2:18*

5. Humankind's mortality. "For who knows what is good for a man in life, during the few and meaningless days he passes through like a shadow? Who can tell him what will happen under the sun after he is gone?" *6:12*

6. How can the meaning of life be discovered? "No one can comprehend what goes on under the sun." *8:17*

7. Everyone dies. "The same destiny overtakes all...afterwards they join the dead." *9:3*

Life lived according to Jesus' ways

1. "Always give yourselves fully to the work of the Lord, because you know that your labor in the Lord is not in vain." *1 Corinthians 15:58*

2. "Therefore, if anyone is in Christ, he is a new creation; the old has gone, the new has come!" *2 Corinthians 5:17*

3. "...he who began a good work in you will carry it on to completion until the day of Christ Jesus." *Philippians 1:6*

4. "...bearing fruit in every good work, growing in the knowledge of God." *Colossians 1:10*

5. "...whoever believes in him shall not perish but have eternal life." *John 3:16*

6. "Now I know in part; then I shall know fully, even as I am fully known." *1 Corinthians 13:12*

7. "God has given us eternal life, and this life is in his Son." *1 John 5:11*

Song of Solomon
FIVE TRUTHS ABOUT TRUE LOVE

The following five truths would enhance any marriage relationship.

Topic	Examples spelled out	Further references in Song of Solomon
1. Delighting in love	"How delightful is your love, my sister, my bride! How much more pleasing is your love than wine" 4:10.	"Let him kiss me with the kisses of his mouth–for your love is more delightful than wine" 1:2. "Take me away with you–let us hurry! Let the king bring me into his chambers" 1:4. "How beautiful you are and how pleasing, O love, with your delights" 7:6.
2. Love's strength	"Place me like a seal over your heart, like a seal over your arm; for love is as strong as death" 8:6.	
3. The commitment of love	"I am my lover's and my lover is mine" 6:3.	"My lover is mine and I am his; he browses among the lilies" 2:16. See also 7:10.
4. The value of love	"If one were to give all the wealth of his house for love, it would be utterly scorned" 8:7.	
5. Don't play with fire	"Daughters of Jerusalem, I charge you: Do not arouse or awaken love until it so desires" 8:4.	"Daughters of Jerusalem, I charge you by the gazelles and by the does of the field: Do not arouse or awaken love until it so desires" 2:7. See also 3:5.

Isaiah

15 PROPHECIES ABOUT JESUS, FULFILLED IN THE NEW TESTAMENT

Prophecy in Isaiah	Fulfilled in the New Testament
	MATTHEW 1:22, 23
7:14 Therefore the Lord himself shall give you a sign; Behold, a virgin shall conceive, and bear a son, and shall call his name Immanuel.	Now all this was done, that it might be fulfilled which was spoken of the Lord by the prophet, saying, Behold, a virgin shall be with child, and shall bring forth a son, and they shall call his name Emmanuel, which being interpreted is, God with us.
	MATTHEW 4:12-16
9:1 Nevertheless the dimness shall not be such as was in her vexation, when at the first he lightly afflicted the land of Zebulun and the land of Naphtali, and afterward did more grievously afflict her by the way of the sea, beyond Jordan, in Galilee of the nations. 9:2 The people that walked in darkness have seen a great light: they that dwell in the land of the shadow of death, upon them hath the light shined.	And leaving Nazareth, he came and dwelt in Capernaum, which is upon the sea coast, in the borders of Zabulon and Nephthalim: That it might be fulfilled which was spoken by Esaias the prophet, saying, The land of Zabulon, and the land of Nephthalim, by the way of the sea, beyond Jordan, Galilee of the Gentiles; The people which sat in darkness saw great light; and to them which sat in the region and shadow of death light is sprung up.
	LUKE 2:11
9:6 For unto us a child is born, unto us a son is given: and the government shall be upon his shoulder: and his name shall be called Wonderful, Counsellor, The mighty God, The everlasting Father, The Prince of Peace.	For unto you is born this day in the city of David a Savior, which is Christ the Lord.
	LUKE 3:22
11:2 And the spirit of the LORD shall rest upon him, the spirit of wisdom and understanding, the spirit of counsel and might, the spirit of knowledge and of the fear of the LORD;	And the Holy Ghost descended in a bodily shape like a dove upon him, and a voice came from heaven, which said, Thou art my beloved Son; in thee I am well pleased.

PETER 2:4-6

28:16 Therefore thus saith the Lord GOD, Behold, I lay in Zion for a foundation a stone, a tried stone, a precious corner stone, a sure foundation: he that believeth shall not make haste.

To whom coming, as unto a living stone, disallowed indeed of men, but chosen of God, and precious, Ye also, as lively stones, are built up a spiritual house, an holy priesthood, to offer up spiritual sacrifices, acceptable to God by Jesus Christ. Wherefore also it is contained in the scripture, Behold, I lay in Sion a chief corner stone, elect, precious; and he that believeth on him shall not be confounded.

MATTHEW 3:1-3

40:3 The voice of him that crieth in the wilderness, Prepare ye the way of the LORD make straight in the desert a highway for our God.

3:1 In those days came John the Baptist, preaching in the wilderness of Judaea,

3:2 And saying, Repent ye: for the kingdom of heaven is at hand.

3:3 For this is he that was spoken of by the prophet Esaias, saying, The voice of one crying in the wilderness, Prepare ye the way of the Lord, make his paths straight.

MATTHEW 12:17-21

42:1 Behold my servant, whom I uphold; mine elect, in whom my soul delighteth; I have put my spirit upon him: he shall bring forth judgment to the Gentiles.

42:2 He shall not cry, nor lift up, nor cause his voice to be heard in the street.

42:3 A bruised reed shall he not break, and the smoking flax shall he not quench: he shall bring forth judgment unto truth.

42:4 He shall not fail nor be discouraged, till he have set judgment in the earth: and the isles shall wait for his law.

12:17 That it might be fulfilled which was spoken by Esaias the prophet, saying,

12:18 Behold my servant, whom I have chosen; my beloved, in whom my soul is well pleased: I will put my spirit upon him, and he shall shew judgment to the Gentiles.

12:19 He shall not strive, nor cry; neither shall any man hear his voice in the streets.

12:20 A bruised reed shall he not break, and smoking flax shall he not quench, till he send forth judgment unto victory.

12:21 And in his name shall the Gentiles trust.

Prophecy in Isaiah	*Fulfilled in the New Testament*
	LUKE 2:29-32
42:6 I the LORD have called thee in righteousness, and will hold thine hand, and will keep thee, and give thee for a covenant of the people, for a light of the Gentiles;	Lord, now lettest thou thou servant depart in peace, according to thy word: For mine eyes have seen thy salvation, Which thou hast prepared before the face of all people; A light to lighten the Gentiles, and the glory of thy people Israel.
	MATTHEW 26:67; 27:26, 30
50:6 I gave my back to the smiters, and my cheeks to them that plucked off the hair: I hid not my face from shame and spitting.	26:67 Then did they spit in his face, and buffeted him; and others smote him with the palms of their hands,
	27:26 Then released he Barabbas unto them: and when he had scourged Jesus, he delivered him to be crucified.
	27:30 And they spit upon him, and took the reed, and smote him on the head.
	PHILIPPIANS 2:7, 8
52:14 As many were astonied at thee; his visage was so marred more than any man, and his form more than the sons of men.	2:7 But made himself of no reputation, and took upon him the form of a servant, and was made in the likeness of men:
	2:8 And being found in fashion as a man, he humbled himself, and became obedient unto death, even the death of the cross.
	ROMANS 5:6, 8
53:4 Surely he hath borne our griefs, and carried our sorrows: yet we did esteem him stricken, smitten of God, and afflicted.	And when we were yet without strength, in due time Christ died for the ungodly.
	But God commendeth his love toward us, in that, while we were yet sinners, Christ died for us.

MATTHEW 27:12-14

53:7 He was oppressed, and he was afflicted, yet he opened not his mouth: he is brought as a lamb to the slaughter, and as a sheep before her shearers is dumb, so he openeth not his mouth.

27:12 And when he was accused of the chief priests and elders, he answered nothing.

27:13 Then said Pilate unto him, Hearest thou not how many things they witness against thee?

27:14 And he answered him to never a word; insomuch that the governor marvelled greatly.

MATTHEW 27:57-60

53:9 And he made his grave with the wicked, and with the rich in his death; because he had done no violence, neither was any deceit in his mouth.

27:57 When the even was come, there came a rich man of Arimathaea, named Joseph, who also himself was Jesus' disciple:

27:58 He went to Pilate, and begged the body of Jesus. Then Pilate commanded the body to be delivered.

27:59 And when Joseph had taken the body, he wrapped it in a clean linen cloth,

27:60 And laid it in his own new tomb, which he had hewn out in the rock: and he rolled a great stone to the door of the sepulchre, and departed.

MARK 15:28

53:12 Therefore will I divide him a portion with the great, and he shall divide the spoil with the strong; because he hath poured out his soul unto death: and he was numbered with the transgressors; and he bare the sin of many, and made intercession for the transgressors.

And the scripture was fulfilled, which saith, And he was numbered with the transgressors.

LUKE 4:18, 19

61:1 The Spirit of the Lord GOD is upon me; because the Lord hath anointed me to preach good tidings unto the meek; he hath sent me to bind up the broken-hearted, to proclaim liberty to the captives, and the opening of the prison to them that are bound.

4:18 The Spirit of the Lord is upon me, because he hath anointed me to preach the gospel to the poor; he hath sent me to heal the brokenhearted, to preach deliverance to the captives, and recovering of sight to the blind, to set at liberty them that are bruised,

4:19 To preach the acceptable year of the Lord.

Jeremiah

TEN RESULTS OF JEREMIAH'S PREACHING

Jeremiah passed on to Judah in his preaching the messages the Lord gave him regardless of the reception his prophecies received.

1. Jeremiah was rejected: 11:18-21.
Plot against Jeremiah

> I had been like a gentle lamb led to the slaughter; I did not realize that they had plotted against me, saying,
> "Let us destroy the tree and its fruit;
> let us cut him off from the land of the living,
> That his name be remembered no more." *11:17-18*

2. Jeremiah as opposed and betrayed by his own family: 12:2-6.
Your brothers

> "Your brothers, your own family–
> even they have betrayed you;
> they have raised a loud cry against you.
> Do not trust them,
> though they speak well of you." *12:6*

3. Jeremiah had to oppose false prophets: 14:13-16; 28:10-17.
False visions

> Then the Lord said to me, "The prophets are prophesying lies in my name. I have not sent them or appointed them or spoken to them. They are prophesying to you false visions, divinations, idolatries and the delusions of their own minds." *14:14*

4. Jeremiah was cursed: 15:10.
Cursed by everyone

> I have neither lent nor borrowed, yet everyone curses me. *15:10*

5. Jeremiah was beaten and put in stocks: 20: 1, 2.
The stocks at the Upper Gate

> When the priest Pashhur son of Immer, the chief officer in the temple of the Lord, heard Jeremiah prophesying these things, he had Jeremiah beaten and put in the stocks at the Upper Gate of Benjamin at the Lord's temple. *20:1-2*

6. Jeremiah was threatened with being killed: 26:8; 36:26.
"You must die!"

> But as soon as Jeremiah finished telling all the people everything the Lord had commanded him to say, the

priests, the prophets and all the people seized him and said, "You must die!" 2 26:8

7. Jeremiah was arrested, detained and accused of being a traitor: 32:2, 3; 37:11-15. "Deserter!"

After the Babylonian army had withdrawn from Jerusalem because of Pharaoh's army, Jeremiah started to leave the city to go to the territory of Benjamin to get his share of the property among the people there. But when he reached the Benjamin Gate, the captain of the guard, whose name was Irijah son of Shelemiah, the son of Hananiah, arrested him and said, "You are deserting to the Babylonians!"

"That's not true!" Jeremiah said. "I am not deserting to the Babylonians." But Irijah would not listen to him; instead, he arrested Jeremiah and brought him to the officials. They were angry with Jeremiah and had him beaten and imprisoned in the house of Jonathan the secretary, which they had made into a prison. 37:11-15

8. Jeremiah had some of his prophecies burned by King Jehoiakim: 36:22-26. The entire scroll was burned

It was the ninth month and the king was sitting in the winter apartment, with a fire burning in the firepot in front of him. Whenever Jehudi had read three or four columns of the scroll, the king cut them off with a scribe's knife and threw them into the firepot, until the entire scroll was burned in the fire. The king and all his attendants who heard all these words showed no fear, nor did they tear their clothes. Even though Elnathan, Delaiah and Gemariah urged the king not to burn the scroll, he would not listen to them. Instead, the king commanded Jerahmeel, a son of the king, Seraiah son of Azriel and Shelemiah son of Abdeel to arrest Baruch the scribe and Jeremiah the prophet. But the Lord had hidden them. 36:22-26

9. Jeremiah was left to die in a cistern: 38:6. Ebed-Melech to the rescue

But Ebed-Melech, a Cushite, an official in the royal palace, heard that they had put Jeremiah into the cistern. While the king was sitting in the Benjamin Gate, Ebed-Melech went out of the palace and said to him, "My lord the king, these men have acted wickedly in all they have done to Jeremiah the prophet. They have thrown him into a cistern, where he will starve to death when there is no longer any bread in the city."

Then the king commanded Ebed-Melech the Cushite, "Take

Lamentations
ITS 22-VERSE-LONG CHAPTERS

Lamentations and poetry

The entire book of Lamentations is poetic and written in a special poetic style which is much more obvious in Hebrew than English. Each chapter is a lament of 22 verses, except for chapter 3, which has 66 verses, 3 times 22.

Acrostic poems

Chapters 1–4 are acrostic poems. Each successive stanza starts with the next letter of the Hebrew alphabet. In chapter 3 the first three verses begin with the letter aleph, the second three with the letter beth, and so on, throughout the 22-letter-long Hebrew alphabet.

It was probably written in this style so that it could be easily used as a funeral song, as it commemorated the destruction of Jerusalem.

thirty men from here with you and lift Jeremiah the prophet out of the cistern before he dies."

So Ebed-Melech took the men with him and went to a room under the treasury in the palace. He took some old rags and worn-out clothes from there and let them down with ropes to Jeremiah in the cistern.

Ebed-Melech the Cushite said to Jeremiah, "Put these old rags and worn-out clothes under your arms to pad the ropes." Jeremiah did so, and they pulled him up with the ropes and lifted him out of the cistern. And Jeremiah remained in the courtyard of the guard. 38:7-13

10. Jeremiah was bound in chains: 40:1. Into exile

The word came to Jeremiah from the Lord after Nebuzaradan commander of the imperial guard had released him at Ramah. He had found Jeremiah bound in chains among all the captives from Jerusalem and Judah who were being carried into exile to Babylon. *40:1*

Ezekiel
16 "I WILL"S

Jesus is seen as the fulfilment of the Shepherd mentioned in Ezekiel chapter 34.

Ezekiel's prophecy in Ezekiel 34:23, "And I will set up one shepherd over them, and he shall feed them, even my servant David; he shall feed them, and he shall be their shepherd" is fulfilled in John 10:11 where Jesus says of himself, "I am the good shepherd. The good shepherd lays down his life for the sheep."

16 prophetic statements
Ezekiel 34:11-31 has 16 prophetic statements which were all fulfilled by Jesus. In each of them note the phrase, "I will."

1. I will search and seek them
For thus saith the Lord GOD; Behold, I, even I, will both search my sheep, and seek them out. *34:11*

2. I will deliver them
As a shepherd seeketh out his flock in the day that he is among his sheep that are scattered; so will I seek out my sheep, and will deliver them out of all places where they have been scattered in the cloudy and dark day. *34:12*

3. I will bring them out
And I will bring them out from the people, and gather them from the countries, and will bring them to their own land, and feed them upon the mountains of Israel by the rivers, and in all the inhabited places of the country. *34:13*

4. I will feed them
I will feed them in a good pasture, and upon the high mountains of Israel shall their fold be: there shall they lie in a good fold, and in a fat pasture shall they feed upon the mountains of Israel. *34:14*

5. I will give them rest
I will feed my flock, and I will cause them to lie down, saith the Lord GOD. *34:15*

6. I will heal them
I will seek that which was lost, and bring again that which was driven away, and will bind up that which was broken, and will strengthen that which was sick: *34:16*

7. I will judge their enemy
but I will destroy the fat and the strong; I will feed them with judgment. *34:16*

8. I will make judgments among my people
And as for you, O my flock, thus saith the Lord GOD; Behold, I judge between cattle and cattle, between the rams and the he goats. *34:17*

Seemeth it a small thing unto you to have eaten up the good pasture, but ye must tread down with your feet the residue of your pastures? and to have drunk of the deep waters, but ye must foul the residue with your feet? *34:18*

And as for my flock, they eat that which ye have trodden with your feet; and they drink that which ye have fouled with your feet. *34:19*

Therefore thus saith the Lord GOD unto them; Behold, I, even I, will judge between the fat cattle and between the lean cattle. *34:20*

Because ye have thrust with side and with shoulder, and pushed all the diseased with your horns, till ye have scattered them abroad; *34:21*

Therefore will I save my flock, and they shall no more be a prey; and I will judge between cattle and cattle. *34:22*

9. I will watch over them
And I will set up one shepherd over them, and he shall feed them, even my servant David; he shall feed them, and he shall be their shepherd. *34:23*

10. I will be their God
And I the LORD will be their God, and my servant David a prince among them; I the LORD have spoken it. *34:24*

11. I will make a covenant of peace
And I will make with them a covenant of peace, and will cause the evil beasts to cease out of the land: *34:25*

12. I will make them live in safety
and they shall dwell safely in the wilderness, and sleep in the woods. *34:25*

13. I will bless them

And I will make them and the places round about my hill a blessing; and I will cause the shower to come down in his season; there shall be showers of blessing. *34:26*

14. They will know me as their Lord
And the tree of the field shall yield her fruit, and the earth shall yield her increase, and they shall be safe in their land, and shall know that I am the LORD, when I have broken the bands of their yoke, and delivered them out of the hand of those that served themselves of them. *34:27*

15. I will make them no longer afraid
And they shall no more be a prey to the heathen, neither shall the beast of the land devour them; but they shall dwell safely, and none shall make them afraid. *34:28*

And I will raise up for them a plant of renown, and they shall be no more consumed with hunger in the land, neither bear the shame of the heathen any more. *34:29*

16. They will know that they are my people
Thus shall they know that I the LORD their God am with them, and that they, even the house of Israel, are my people, saith the Lord GOD. *34:30*

And ye my flock, the flock of my pasture, are men, and I am your God, saith the Lord GOD. *34:31*

Daniel

FIVE MIRACLES IN DANIEL

There are five unusual events or miracles in Daniel's book:

1. God revealed to Daniel the dream and the interpretation of the dream Nebuchadnezzar had forgotten: 2:1-47.
2. Shadrach, Meshach, and Abednego were saved from being killed in the fiery furnace: 3:19-28.
3. God made Nebuchadnezzar eat grass like a wild animal to humble him, and then restored him: 4:24-37.
4. Writing on the wall appeared during Belshazzar's great feast: 5:1-31.
5. God protected Daniel when he spent a night in the lions' den: 6:1-28.

Hosea

16 WAYS IN WHICH EPHRAIM SINNED AGAINST GOD

Ephraim

Ephraim became a byword and symbol of Israel's sin. Hosea knew that the best way to deal with sin was to expose it, so that it could be confessed to God, and turned away from. Hosea indicates the numerous ways in which Ephraim sinned against God.

1. Ephraim joined herself to idols: 4:17.
2. Ephraim failed to acknowledge God: 5:4.
3. Ephraim was arrogant: 5:5.
4. Ephraim was unfaithful: 5:7.
5. Ephraim turned to godless people (Assyria) for help: 5:13.
6. Ephraim's love for God was like the dew: 6:4.
7. Ephraim's unfaithfulness to God was like the unfaithfulness of a prostitute: 6:10.
8. Ephraim does not search for God: 7:10.
9. Ephraim lied against God: 7:13.
10. Ephraim did not pray to God from her heart: 7:14.
11. Ephraim plotted evil against God: 7:15.
12. Ephraim rejected what is good: 8:3.
13. Ephraim bears no fruit: 9:16.
14. Ephraim did not acknowledge God's goodness: 11:3.
15. Ephraim turned away from God: 11:7.
16. Ephraim sinned more and more: 13:2.

Joel

FIVE WAYS TO TURN TO GOD

In Joel's prophecy Joel frequently urges his hearers to turn back to God in repentance:

"Therefore also now, saith the LORD, turn ye even to me with all your heart, and with fasting, and with weeping, and with mourning:

And rend your heart, and not your garments, and turn unto the LORD your God: for he is gracious and merciful, slow to anger, and of great kindness, and repenteth him of the evil.

Who knoweth if he will return and repent, and leave a blessing behind him; even a meat offering and a drink offering unto the LORD your God?

Blow the trumpet in Zion, sanctify a fast, call a solemn assembly:

Gather the people, sanctify the congregation, assemble the elders, gather the children, and those that suck the breasts: let the bridegroom go forth of his chamber, and the bride out of her closet.

Let the priests, the ministers of the LORD, weep between the porch and the altar, and let them say, Spare thy people, O LORD, and give not thine heritage to reproach, that the heathen should rule over them: wherefore should they say among the people, Where is their God?" 2:12-17

1. The direction in which to turn: turn to God: 12a
2. Turn wholeheartedly: 12b
3. Turn and fast: 12c
4. Turn with tears of repentance: 12d
5. Turn in your interior: 13

Amos

SIX ILLUSTRATIONS TO LEARN FROM

Amos loved to illustrated his prophecies with homely figures of speech.	
Illustration	**Message**
1. A cart fully laden with grain	As such a cart crushes everything in its path, so the Lord will crush you. 3:8
2. A roaring lion...	...is like his own call to be a prophet. 3:8
3. Two leg bones and a piece of a sheep's ear is rescued from a lion's mouth	This is a picture of Israel being rescued. 3:12
4. Empty stomachs	Famine will come. 4:6
5. A plumbline	A plumbline of truth reveal Israel's crooked ways. 7:7, 8
6. A basket of ripe fruit	Israel is about to be judged. 8:1-3

Obadiah

EIGHT RESULTS OF EDOM'S PRIDE

The prophecy of Obadiah is one of the clearest biblical examples of pride going before a fall (see 1 Corinthians 10:12).

Because of its arrogance and cruelty towards Judah, Edom will fall:

1. "I will make you small among the nations." (2)
2. "The pride of your heart has deceived you." (3)
3. "Oh, what a disaster awaits you." (5)
4. "How Esau will be ransacked." (6)
5. "Your warriors, O Teman, will be terrified." (9)
6. "You will be covered with shame." (10)
7. "You will be destroyed forever." (10)
8. "Your deeds will return upon your own head." (15)

Jonah

FIVE THINGS TO LEARN FROM THE BOOK OF JONAH

1. We learn about God

a. God is just

The whole book assumes that God is just. Everyone is answerable to God, not just Israel.

See 1:2; 3:2, 9, 10.

b. God is sovereign

God is not only the Creator but controls his world, including the weather, his creatures and plants.

See 1:4, 9, 17; 2:10.

c. God is compassionate

God is full of mercy and compassion. This extends beyond Israel to all nations, and even to animals.

See 2:8, 9; 3:9, 10; 4:2, 10, 11.

2. We learn about Jonah

Jonah is a representative of God's people.

Jonah had experienced God's love and grace. He prayed to God. He praised God and recommitted his life to God.

See 1:3, 10; 4:1-3, 9.

3. We learn about pagan nations

Although Jonah had no time for them because they were not Israelites God was concerned for them. They display a sense of right and wrong and repent.

See 1:13, 14, 16; 3:5-9.

Micah

12 SINS TO AVOID

Micah speaks out against the evil practices of both Israel and Judah. He accuses them of 12 sins:

1. Idolatory. "All her idols will be broken to pieces" 1:7.
2. Hatching evil plots. "Woe to those who plan iniquity" 2:1.
3. Covetousness. "They covet fields and seize them" 2:2a.
4. Fraud. "They defraud a man of his home" 2:2b.
5. Murder. "...who tear the skin from my people" 3:2.
6. Following false prophets. "...the prophets who lead my people astray" 3:5.
7. Witchcraft. "I will destroy your witchcraft" 5:12.
8. Dishonesty. "Shall I acquit a man with dishonest scales?" 6:11.
9. Violence. "Her rich men are violent" 6:12.
10. Lying. "Her people are liars" 6:12.
11. Being open to bribery. "The judge accepts bribes" 7:3.
12. Family break-ups. "...a son dishonors his father" 7:6.

Nahum

EIGHT DETAILS ABOUT THE FALL OF NINEVEH

While Jonah was called to preach a message of repentance to Nineveh, Nahum's prophecy is about God's judgment on Nineveh. God had "lost patience" with the city of Nineveh. Nahum gives specific details about how Nineveh will be overthrown. All these events have been confirmed by historical accounts and archeological finds.

1. Nineveh will be destroyed by a flood, 1:8; 2:6.
2. Nineveh will be destroyed by fire, 1:10; 2:13; 3:13, 15.
3. Nineveh's images and temples will be destroyed, 1:14.
4. Nineveh will never be rebuilt, 1:14; 2:11, 13.
5. Nineveh's leaders will run away, 3:17.
6. Nineveh will be under siege, 3:14.
7. Nineveh's city gates will be destroyed, 3:13.
8. Nineveh will attempt to strengthen its defences, 3:14.

Habakkuk

FIVE WOES OF HABAKKUK

Habakkuk sees injustice and violence on every side in his native Judah and pronounces God's judgment on these evil practices.

The five woes

1. Against extortion. "Woe to him who…makes himself wealthy by extortion" 2:6.
2. Against dishonesty. "Woe to him who builds his realm by unjust gain" 2:9.
3. Against violence and crime. "Woe to him who builds a city with bloodshed and establishes a town by crime!" 2:12.
4. Against drunkenness. "Woe to him who gives drink to his neighbors, pouring it from the wineskin till they are drunk" 2:15.
5. Against idolatry. "Woe to him who says to wood, 'Come to life!' Or to lifeless stone, 'Wake up!' Can it give guidance?" 2:19.

Zephaniah

SEVEN OF GOD'S BLESSINGS

WHAT GOD HAS DONE FOR JUDAH	
Zephaniah ends his prophecy by telling Judah that God will have mercy on all who seek him.	
Reference in Zephaniah	*Link verse*
1. Judgment is removed 3:15a	Isaiah 53:6
2. Enemy is defeated 3:15b	Ephesians 1:20-23
3. Brought them close to God 3:15c	Ephesians 2:13-18
4. Taken fear away 3:16	1 John 4:18
5. Delivered from the enemy 3:17a	2 Corinthians 1:9, 10
6. Delighted in them 3:17b	Romans 5:11
7. Bestowed his love on them 17c	Hebrews 1:1-3

Haggai

FIVE BLESSINGS GIVEN AS WE WORK FOR GOD

Haggai encourages God's people who have now returned from exile to rebuild the temple in Jerusalem. He reminds them of how God will bless them as they do God's work.

1. God's presence is promised. "Be strong...and work. For I am with you" 2:4.
2. God's Spirit is with them. "And my Spirit remains among you" 2:5.
3. Fear is banished. "Do not fear" 2:5.
4. Overwhelms them with his glory. "I will fill this house with glory" 2:7.
5. God's peace is promised. "...in this place I will grant peace" 2:9.

Zechariah

TEN CHARACTERISTICS OF THE COMING MESSIAH

Zechariah's prophesies foretell details about Jesus coming as the Messiah.

1. His coming will be humble: 6:12.
2. He refers to the Messiah's humanity: 13:7.
3. He mentions his rejection and betrayal for 30 pieces of silver: 11:12, 13.
4. His crucifixion: 13:7.
5. His priesthood: 6:13.
6. His kingship: "Rejoice greatly, O Daughter of Zion! Shout, Daughter of Jerusalem! See your king comes to you, righteous and having salvation" 9:9.
7. His coming in glory: 14:3, 4.
8. He will build the Lord's temple: 6:12, 13
9. He will reign: "His rule will extend from sea to sea" 9:10.
10. He will usher in a time of peace: "In that day each of you will invite his neighbor to sit under his vine and fig-tree" 3:10.

Malachi

SEVEN CHARACTERISTICS OF A TRUE WORKER FOR GOD

Malachi tells the godly remnant how they should serve God.

1. Their state of mind: They should fear God. "This called for reverence" 2:5.
2. Their message: They should proclaim the truth. "True instruction was in his mouth" 2:6.
3. Their purity: They avoided sin. "Nothing false was found on his lips" 2:6.
4. Their relationship with God: They walked with God. "He walked with me in peace" 2:6.
5. Their work for God: They turned people back to God. "...turned many from sin" 2:6.
6. Their duty: They taught God's law and his instructions. "For the lips of a priest ought to preserve knowledge" 2:7.
7. Their commission: They were God's messengers. "...because he is the messenger of the Lord Almighty" 2:7.

4 FASCINATING FEATURES ABOUT INDIVIDUAL NEW TESTAMENT BOOKS

Introduction

Each one of the four Gospels has passages and features that are unique to that Gospel alone. Chapter 4 begins by looking at what can be learnt from these features.

Most of us tend to read and re-read favorite parts of the New Testament. We may rarely stray into the less familiar territory of the second and third letters of John, or the book of Jude. These 27 studies – one study for each New Testament book – give a balanced picture of the whole of the New Testament.

It is sometimes maintained that Christians should jettison the Old Testament and study only the New but this is not a view taken by the New Testament itself. Two of these studies therefore emphasize the links between the Old and New Testaments: the 54 Old Testament references found in Romans, and the ten examples of faith in Hebrews.

Perhaps a less common way of studying a feature of a New Testament book comes in three of these studies, which show how one particular Bible book links up with other teaching from within the New Testament. In James' letter and in Peter's first letter nine similarities between the teaching of Jesus and that of James and Peter are found, while 23 comparisons between 1 John and John's Gospel are touched on in studying John's first letter.

Matthew

23 THINGS ONLY RECORDED BY MATTHEW

Unique to Matthew

When the other three Gospels, Mark, Luke and John, are compared with Matthew, 23 things stand out as being unique to Matthew.

1. The descent of Christ through Joseph.

"...and Jacob the father of Joseph, the husband of Mary, of whom was born Jesus, who is called Christ" 1:16.

2.The visit of the wise men to the infant Jesus.

2:1-12.

3. Joseph, Mary and the infant Jesus fleeing to Egypt.

"He [Joseph] got up, took the child and his mother during the night and left for Egypt" 2:14.

4. Herod's murder of the children around Bethlehem.

"Herod...gave orders to kill all the boys in Bethlehem and its vicinity who were two years old and under" 2:16.

5. Jesus and his family settling down in Nazareth.

"He [Joseph] got up, took the child and his mother and...went and lived in a town called Nazareth" 2:22.

6. The Pharisees and the Sadducees observe John the Baptist.

"But when he saw many of the Pharisees and Sadducees coming to where he was baptizing, he said to them: 'You brood of vipers!'" 3:7.

7. The sermon on the mount: chapters 5–7.

"And seeing the multitudes, he went up into a mountain: and when he was set, his disciples came unto him: And he opened his mouth, and taught them, saying,

Blessed are the poor in spirit: for theirs is the kingdom of heaven.

Blessed are they that mourn: for they shall be comforted.

Blessed are the meek: for they shall inherit the earth.

Blessed are they which do hunger and thirst after righteousness: for they shall be filled.

Blessed are the merciful: for they shall obtain mercy.

Blessed are the pure in heart: for they shall see God.

Blessed are the peacemakers: for they shall be called the children of God.

Blessed are they which are persecuted for righteousness' sake: for theirs is the kingdom of heaven.

Blessed are ye, when men shall revile you, and persecute you, and shall say all manner of evil against you falsely, for my sake.

Rejoice, and be exceeding glad: for great is your reward in heaven: for so persecuted they the prophets which were before you" *5:1-12 KJV*

8. Jesus healing two blind men.

9:27-31.

9.Jesus healing the demon-possessed mute man.

9:32-33.

10. Jesus' invitation to take rest from him and his yoke.

"Come unto me, all ye that labor and are heavy laden, and I will give you rest.

Take my yoke upon you, and learn of me; for I am meek and lowly in heart: and ye shall find rest unto your souls.

For my yoke is easy, and my burden is light" *11:28-30 KJV*

11. Jesus healing the sick he had compassion on.

"When Jesus landed and saw a large crowd, he had compassion on them and healed their sick" 14:14.

12. Peter walking on the water.

"Then Peter got down out of the boat, walked on the water and came towards Jesus" 14:29.

13. Jesus paying the temple tax with a coin from a fish's mouth.

"And when they were come to Capernaum, they that received tribute money came to Peter, and said, Doth not your master pay tribute?

He saith, Yes. And when he was come into the house, Jesus prevented him, saying, What thinkest thou, Simon? of whom do the kings of the earth take custom or tribute? of their own children, or of strangers?

Peter saith unto him, Of strangers.

Jesus saith unto him, Then are the children free.

Notwithstanding, lest we should offend them, go thou to the sea, and cast an hook, and take up the fish that first cometh up; and when thou hast opened his mouth, thou shalt find a piece of money: that take, and give unto them for me and thee" *17:24-27 KJV*

14. Denouncing the Pharisees.

23:1-39.

15. The amount of money paid to Judas for betraying Jesus.

"So they counted out for him [Judas] thirty silver coins" 26:15.

16. Judas returning the 30 silver coins.

27:1-10.

17. The dream Pilate's wife had.

"While Pilate was sitting on the judge's seat, his wife sent him this message: 'Don't have anything to do with that innocent man, for I have suffered a great deal today in a dream because of him'" 27:19.

18. The people who were raised to life immediately after Jesus' death.

"The tombs broke open and the bodies of many holy people who had died were raised to life" 27:52.

19. Pilate agreeing to Roman soldiers guarding Jesus' tomb.

27:64-66.

20. The earthquake at Jesus' resurrection.

"There was a violent earthquake, for an angel of the Lord came down from heaven…" 28:2.

21. The chief priests bribe the soldiers to lie about Jesus' body being stolen.

"Now when they were going, behold, some of the watch came into the city, and shewed unto the chief priests all the things that were done.

And when they were assembled with the elders, and had taken counsel, they gave large money unto the soldiers,

Saying, Say ye, His disciples came by night, and stole him away while we slept.

And if this come to the governor's ears, we will persuade him, and secure you.

So they took the money, and did as they were taught: and this saying is commonly reported among the Jews until this day." *28:11-15 KJV*

22. Jesus giving the great commission.

"And Jesus came and spake unto them, saying, …Go ye therefore, and teach all nations, baptizing them in the name of the Father, and of the Son, and of the Holy Ghost." *28:18, 19*

23. LIST OF 12 PARABLES UNIQUE TO MATTHEW			
	Name	*Reference*	*Lesson to draw from parable*
1.	The weeds	13:24-30, 36-43	Good and evil in life and judgment
2.	The hidden treasure	13:44	The value of the gospel
3.	The only valuable pearl	13:45, 46	Seek salvation
4.	The net and fish	13:47-50	The visible members of the church
5.	Clean and unclean food	15:10-20	Inward purity
6.	The unforgiving servant	18:23-55	Ingratitude
7.	Workers in the vineyard	20:1-16	Being faithful to God's call
8.	The two sons	21:28-32	Insincerity and repentance
9.	The marriage party	22:2-14	Need for God's righteousness
10.	The ten virgins	25:1-13	Be prepared and alert
11.	The talents	25:14-30	Use your gifts
12.	The sheep and the goats	25:31-46	Judgment and separation of good and bad

Mark

19 NAMES AND TITLES OF JESUS

Mark uses 19 titles to describe Jesus. It is instructive to see who used which title of Jesus and on what occasion.

Son of Man

Listed are the first occurrence of each of the titles Mark used of Jesus.

Go through Mark's Gospel and see who uses the title "Son of Man" and why this title is used.

Five titles of God

1. Father: 8:38
2. The God of Abraham, the God of Isaac, the God of Jacob: 12:26
3. Lord: 12:29
4. Abba: 14:36

Two titles of the Holy Spirit

1. The Holy Spirit: 1:8
2. The Spirit: 1:10

Miracles and parables unique to Mark

Miracles unique to Mark

1. Deaf and mute man cured, 7:31-37
2. Blind man cured, 8:22-26

Parables unique to Mark

1. Fasting, 2:19, 20. "How can the guests of the bridegroom fast while he is still with them? They cannot so long as he is with them. But the time will come when the bridegroom will be taken away from them, and on that day they will fast."
2. Seed growing secretly, 4:26-29

19 TITLES OF JESUS	
Title	*Reference*
1. Jesus Christ	1:1
2. Son of God	1:1
3. Lord	1:3
4. Beloved Son (*KJV*) My Son whom I love	1:11
5. Jesus of Nazareth	1:24
6. Holy One of God	1:24
7. Son of Man	2:10
8. Lord of the Sabbath	2:28
9. Teacher	4:38
10. Jesus	5:7
11. Son of the Most High God	5:7
12. The carpenter	6:3
13. The Christ	8:29
14. Good teacher	10:17
15. Son of David	10:47
16. Son of the Blessed One	14:61
17. King of the Jews	15:2
18. King of Israel	15:32
19. Jesus the Nazarene	16:6

Luke

17 PARABLES UNIQUE TO LUKE

The complete Gospel

Luke has been called the most complete Gospel in the sense that he records more news about people, more about Jesus' resurrection and more parables than the other Gospels.

Without Luke's Gospel we would not know about 17 of Jesus' parables.

Interpreting parables

Studying the parables is a most fruitful Bible study. Work out why you think

Jesus told the three printed parables.

Details

It is easy to misinterpret parables. There are a few pitfalls to avoid. The details Jesus gives are not unimportant. However, beware of giving them a meaning that may never have been intended.

To whom was the parable originally spoken?

There are certain clues which give the

17 PARABLES		
Name	*Reference*	*Lesson to draw from parable*
1. Two debtors	7:41-43	Be grateful for pardon
2. Good Samaritan	10:30-37	Compassion on people in need
3. Neighbor in need	11:5-8	Persevere in prayer
4. The lamp	11:33-36	Open witness
5. The rich fool	12:16-21	A mind in the grip of this world
6. The wedding party	12:35-40	Be on the look-out for Jesus' return
7. The wise manager	12:42-48	Be worthy of trust
8. The fruitless fig-tree	13:6-9	Being useless, despite grace
9. Guests at a wedding banquet	14:7-15	Humility
10. The great banquet	14:16-24	God's call to everyone
11. The lost coin	15:8-10	Joy over repentance
12. The runaway son	15:11-32	God's fatherly love
13. The shrewd manager	16:1-13	Preparing for eternity
14. The unworthy servant	17:7-10	God's claim on us to serve him
15. The widow and the judge	18:1-8	Need for persistent faith
16. Pharisee and tax-collector	18:9-14	Self-righteousness and humility
17. The servant and the ten minas	19:11-27	Diligence and laziness contrasted

correct interpretation of each parable. Note to whom Jesus addressed the parable. Also see if the context of the passage gives you any information about the background to the parable.

The punch-line
Jesus sometimes ended his parables with a punch-line, or conclusion. Look and see if he did and if so what should be drawn from this.

Reactions
The Gospel writers sometimes include a reaction to a parable Jesus told which can also shed light on the meaning of the parable.

One main point
In the parable of the runaway son there is an important lesson to be drawn from the reaction of the elder son. However, in most parables, there is only one main point. Work out what you think this is for each parable.

Three of Luke's parables to study
The Good Samaritan

And, behold, a certain lawyer stood up, and tempted him, saying, Master, what shall I do to inherit eternal life?

He said unto him, What is written in the law? how readest thou?

And he answering said, Thou shalt love the Lord thy God with all thy heart, and with all thy soul, and with all thy strength, and with all thy mind; and thy neighbor as thyself.

And he said unto him, Thou hast answered right: this do, and thou shalt live.

But he, willing to justify himself, said unto Jesus, And who is my neighbor?

And Jesus answering said, A certain man went down from Jerusalem to Jericho, and fell among thieves, which stripped him of his raiment, and wounded him, and departed, leaving him half dead.

And by chance there came down a certain priest that way: and when he saw him, he passed by on the other side.

And likewise a Levite, when he was at the place, came and looked on him, and passed by on the other side.

But a certain Samaritan, as he journeyed, came where he was: and when he saw him, he had compassion on him,

And went to him, and bound up his wounds, pouring in oil and wine, and set him on his own beast, and brought him to an inn, and took care of him.

And on the morrow when he departed, he took out two pence, and gave them to the host, and said unto him, Take care of him; and whatsoever thou spendest more, when I come again, I will repay thee.

Which now of these three, thinkest

thou, was neighbor unto him that fell among the thieves?

And he said, He that shewed mercy on him. Then said Jesus unto him, Go, and do thou likewise.

Luke 10:25-37 KJV

The runaway son

Then drew near unto him all the publicans and sinners for to hear him.

And the Pharisees and scribes murmured, saying, This man receiveth sinners, and eateth with them...

And he said, A certain man had two sons:

And the younger of them said to his father, Father, give me the portion of goods that falleth to me. And he divided unto them his living.

And not many days after the younger son gathered all together, and took his journey into a far country, and there wasted his substance with riotous living.

And when he had spent all, there arose a mighty famine in that land; and he began to be in want.

And he went and joined himself to a citizen of that country; and he sent him into his fields to feed swine.

And he would fain have filled his belly with the husks that the swine did eat: and no man gave unto him.

And when he came to himself, he said, How many hired servants of my father's have bread enough and to spare, and I perish with hunger!

I will arise and go to my father, and will say unto him, Father, I have sinned against heaven, and before thee,

And am no more worthy to be called thy son: make me as one of thy hired servants.

And he arose, and came to his father. But when he was yet a great way off, his father saw him, and had compassion, and ran, and fell on his neck, and kissed him.

And the son said unto him, Father, I have sinned against heaven, and in thy sight, and am no more worthy to be called thy son.

But the father said to his servants, Bring forth the best robe, and put it on him; and put a ring on his hand, and shoes on his feet:

And bring hither the fatted calf, and kill it; and let us eat, and be merry:

For this my son was dead, and is alive again; he was lost, and is found. And they began to be merry.

Now his elder son was in the field: and as he came and drew nigh to the house, he heard musick and dancing.

And he called one of the servants, and asked what these things meant.

And he said unto him, Thy brother is come; and thy father hath killed the fatted calf, because he hath received him safe and sound.

And he was angry, and would not go

in: therefore came his father out, and intreated him.

And he answering said to his father, Lo, these many years do I serve thee, neither transgressed I at any time thy commandment: and yet thou never gavest me a kid, that I might make merry with my friends:

But as soon as this thy son was come, which hath devoured thy living with harlots, thou hast killed for him the fatted calf.

And he said unto him, Son, thou art ever with me, and all that I have is thine.

It was meet that we should make merry, and be glad: for this thy brother was dead, and is alive again; and was lost, and is found.

Luke 15:1, 2, 11-32 KJV

The Pharisee and the tax-collector

And he spake this parable unto certain which trusted in themselves that they were righteous, and despised others:

Two men went up into the temple to pray; the one a Pharisee, and the other a publican.

The Pharisee stood and prayed thus with himself, God, I thank thee, that I am not as other men are, extortioners, unjust, adulterers, or even as this publican.

I fast twice in the week, I give tithes of all that I possess.

And the publican, standing afar off, would not lift up so much as his eyes unto heaven, but smote upon his breast, saying, God be merciful to me a sinner.

I tell you, this man went down to his house justified rather than the other: for every one that exalteth himself shall be abased; and he that humbleth himself shall be exalted.

Luke 18:9-14 KJV

John

12 DISCOURSES ONLY RECORDED BY JOHN

John does not record any parables in his Gospel. However, he does include a number of discourses spoken by Jesus which are unique to his Gospel.

Ten discourses

John collected ten discourses which Jesus either made in public or which were given to individuals.

1. Nicodemus and the new birth: 3:1-21
2. The woman of Samaria and everlasting life: 4:5-21
3. Life in Jesus: 5:19-47
4. The bread of life: 6:29-59
5. The source of truth: 7:14-29
6. The light of the world: 8:12-20
7. Trusting Jesus: 8:21-30
8. Freedom: 8:31-59
9. The good shepherd: 10:1-18
10. Jesus united to his Father: 10:22-28

Two discourses

John records two discourses which he gave to his disciples in private.

1. Jesus' death: 12:20-36
2. Teaching about discipleship: 13:31–16:6

Allegories

While John has no parables in his Gospel he does have a number of allegories which Jesus also used to teach truths about himself. There are important lessons about Jesus and about salvation to be gleaned from the following allegory. It is also instructive to note the reactions people had to this allegory.

Jesus as the good shepherd
The allegory

Verily, verily, I say unto you, He that entereth not by the door into the sheepfold, but climbeth up some other way, the same is a thief and a robber.
But he that entereth in by the door is the shepherd of the sheep.
To him the porter openeth; and the sheep hear his voice: and he calleth his own sheep by name, and leadeth them out.
And when he putteth forth his own sheep, he goeth before them, and the sheep follow him: for they know his voice.
And a stranger will they not follow, but will flee from him: for they know not the voice of strangers.
This parable spake Jesus unto them: but they understood not what things they were which he spake unto them.
Then said Jesus unto them again, Verily, verily, I say unto you, I am the door of the sheep.
All that ever came before me are thieves and robbers: but the sheep did not hear them.
I am the door: by me if any man enter in, he shall be saved, and shall go in and out, and find pasture.
The thief cometh not, but for to steal, and to kill, and to destroy: I am come that they might have life, and that they might have it more abundantly.

I am the good shepherd: the good shepherd giveth his life for the sheep.

But he that is an hireling, and not the shepherd, whose own the sheep are not, seeth the wolf coming, and leaveth the sheep, and fleeth: and the wolf catcheth them, and scattereth the sheep.

The hireling fleeth, because he is an hireling, and careth not for the sheep.

I am the good shepherd, and know my sheep, and am known of mine.

As the Father knoweth me, even so know I the Father: and I lay down my life for the sheep.

And other sheep I have, which are not of this fold: them also I must bring, and they shall hear my voice; and there shall be one fold, and one shepherd.

Therefore doth my Father love me, because I lay down my life, that I might take it again.

No man taketh it from me, but I lay it down of myself. I have power to lay it down, and I have power to take it again. This commandment have I received of my Father.

Reactions to the allegory

There was a division therefore again among the Jews for these sayings.

And many of them said, He hath a devil, and is mad; why hear ye him?

Others said, These are not the words of him that hath a devil. Can a devil open the eyes of the blind?

John 10:1-21 KJV

Acts

29 MIRACLES

The book of miracles

After the four Gospels comes the book of Acts, which has been given various names, such as:

- The Acts
- The Acts of the Apostles
- The Acts of the Holy Spirit
- The History of the Early Church
- The Book of Christian Action

It records more miracles than any other New Testament book.

1. The coming of the Holy Spirit: 2:1-4
2. The gift of tongues: 2:4
3. The sudden death of Ananias and Sapphira: 5:1-11
4. The apostles' release from prison: 5:19, 20
5. Stephen's miracles: 6:8
6. Stephen's vision of Jesus: 7:55, 56
7. Philip's miracles: 8:6
8. Jesus appearing to Saul on the Damascus road: 9:1-6
9. Saul's sight restored: 9:15-22
10. Cornelius' vision: 10:1-8, 30-32
11. Peter's vision: 10:9-48

Peter and Cornelius

There are at least three miracles to note in this passage.

Cornelius' vision

There was a certain man in Caesarea called Cornelius, a centurion of the band called the Italian band, A devout man, and one that feared God with all his house, which gave much alms to the people, and prayed to God alway.

He saw in a vision evidently about the ninth hour of the day an angel of God coming in to him, and saying unto him, Cornelius.

And when he looked on him, he was afraid, and said, What is it, Lord? And he said unto him, Thy prayers and thine alms are come up for a memorial before God.

And now send men to Joppa, and call for one Simon, whose surname is Peter:

He lodgeth with one Simon a tanner, whose house is by the sea side: he shall tell thee what thou oughtest to do.

And when the angel which spake unto Cornelius was departed, he called two of his household servants, and a devout soldier of them that waited on him continually;

And when he had declared all these things unto them, he sent them to Joppa.

Peter's vision

On the morrow, as they went on their journey, and drew nigh unto the city, Peter went up upon the housetop to pray about the sixth hour:

And he became very hungry, and would have eaten: but while they made ready, he fell into a trance,

And saw heaven opened, and a certain vessel descending upon him, as it

had been a great sheet knit at the
four corners, and let down to the
earth:

Wherein were all manner of fourfooted
beasts of the earth, and wild beasts,
and creeping things, and fowls of the
air.

And there came a voice to him, Rise,
Peter; kill, and eat.

But Peter said, Not so, Lord; for I have
never eaten any thing that is
common or unclean.

And the voice spake unto him again
the second time, What God hath
cleansed, that call not thou common.

This was done thrice: and the vessel
was received up again into heaven.

Now while Peter doubted in himself
what this vision which he had seen
should mean, behold, the men
which were sent from Cornelius had
made enquiry for Simon's house, and
stood before the gate, And called,
and asked whether Simon, which
was surnamed Peter, were lodged
there.

While Peter thought on the vision, the
Spirit said unto him, Behold, three
men seek thee.

Arise therefore, and get thee down,
and go with them, doubting nothing:
for I have sent them.

Then Peter went down to the men
which were sent unto him from
Cornelius; and said, Behold, I am he
whom ye seek: what is the cause
wherefore ye are come?

And they said, Cornelius the
centurion, a just man, and one that
feareth God, and of good report
among all the nation of the Jews,
was warned from God by an holy
angel to send for thee into his house,
and to hear words of thee.

Then called he them in, and lodged
them. And on the morrow Peter
went away with them, and certain
brethren from Joppa accompanied
him.

And the morrow after they entered into
Caesarea. And Cornelius waited for
them, and he had called together his
kinsmen and near friends.

The miracle following Peter's preaching

And as Peter was coming in, Cornelius
met him, and fell down at his feet,
and worshiped him.

But Peter took him up, saying, Stand
up; I myself also am a man.

And as he talked with him, he went in,
and found many that were come
together.

And he said unto them, Ye know how
that it is an unlawful thing for a man
that is a Jew to keep company, or
come unto one of another nation;
but God hath shewed me that I
should not call any man common or
unclean.

Therefore came I unto you without
gainsaying, as soon as I was sent for:
I ask therefore for what intent ye
have sent for me?

And Cornelius said, Four days ago I was fasting until this hour; and at the ninth hour I prayed in my house, and, behold, a man stood before me in bright clothing,

And said, Cornelius, thy prayer is heard, and thine alms are had in remembrance in the sight of God.

Send therefore to Joppa, and call hither Simon, whose surname is Peter; he is lodged in the house of one Simon a tanner by the sea side: who, when he cometh, shall speak unto thee.

Immediately therefore I sent to thee; and thou hast well done that thou art come. Now therefore are we all here present before God, to hear all things that are commanded thee of God.

Then Peter opened his mouth, and said, Of a truth I perceive that God is no respecter of persons:

But in every nation he that feareth him, and worketh righteousness, is accepted with him.

The word which God sent unto the children of Israel, preaching peace by Jesus Christ: (he is Lord of all:)

That word, I say, ye know, which was published throughout all Judaea, and began from Galilee, after the baptism which John preached;

How God anointed Jesus of Nazareth with the Holy Ghost and with power: who went about doing good, and healing all that were oppressed of the devil; for God was with him.

And we are witnesses of all things which he did both in the land of the Jews, and in Jerusalem; whom they slew and hanged on a tree:

Him God raised up the third day, and shewed him openly;

Not to all the people, but unto witnesses chosen before God, even to us, who did eat and drink with him after he rose from the dead.

And he commanded us to preach unto the people, and to testify that it is he which was ordained of God to be the

Judge of quick and dead.

To him give all the prophets witness, that through his name whosoever believeth in him shall receive remission of sins.

While Peter yet spake these words, the Holy Ghost fell on all them which heard the word.

And they of the circumcision which believed were astonished, as many as came with Peter, because that on the Gentiles also was poured out the gift of the Holy Ghost.

For they heard them speak with tongues, and magnify God. Then answered Peter,

Can any man forbid water, that these should not be baptized, which have received the Holy Ghost as well as we?

And he commanded them to be baptized in the name of the Lord. Then prayed they him to tarry certain days. *Acts 10 KJV*

12. Agabus' prophecy about a famine: 11:28
13. Paul and Barnabas' miracles: 14:3
14. Paul's survival after been stoned: 14:19, 20
15. Paul's Macedonian vision: 16:9
16. The earthquake at Philippi: 16:25-31
17. Seven sons of Sceva overpowered: 19:13-16
18. Agabus' prophecy about Paul: 21:10, 11
19. Paul not harmed by viper's bite: 28:3-5

Four miracles by the hand of Peter

20. A lame man cured: 3:7
21. Healing the sick: 5:15, 16
22. Aeneas healed: 9:33, 34
23. Dorcas brought back to life: 9:36-40

Six miracles by the hand of Paul

24. Elymas made blind: 13:11
25. Lame man healed: 14:10
26. Spirit expelled from slave girl: 16:18
27. Extraordinary miracles at Ephesus: 19:11
28. Eutychus brought back to life: 20:10-12
29. Publius' father healed: 28:8, 9

Romans

54 EXAMPLES OF THE OLD TESTAMENT IN ROMANS

PAUL'S USE OF THE OLD TESTAMENT		
In his letter to the Romans Paul either quotes from or makes allusions to over 60 Old Testament verses. He bases the theme of this whole letter on a quotation from Habakkuk:		
Romans	*Old Testament*	*Theme*
1. 1:17	Habukkuk 2:4	The righteous will live by faith
2. 2:24	Isaiah 52:5	God's name is blasphemed
3. 3:4	Psalm 51:4	Proved right when you speak
4. 3:10	Psalm 14:1, 3	No one is righteous
5. 3:11	Psalm 14:2	No one understands
6. 3:12	Psalm 14:3	All have turned away
7. 3:13	Psalm 5:9	Their throats are open graves
8. 3:14	Psalm 10:7	Mouths are full of cursing
9. 3:15	Isaiah 59:7	Feet are swift to shed blood
10. 3:16	Isaiah 59:8	Ruin and misery
11. 3:18	Psalm 36:1	No fear of God
12. 4:3	Genesis 15:6	Abraham's belief in God
13. 4:7	Psalm 32:1, 2	Sins forgiven
14. 4:18	Genesis 15:5	Abraham father of many nations
15. 7:7	Exodus 20:17	Do not covet
16. 8:36	Psalm 44:22	Facing death all day long
17. 9:7	Genesis 21:12	Offspring will be reckoned through Isaac
18. 9:9	Genesis 18:10	Sarah will have a son
19. 9:12	Genesis 25:23	The older will serve the younger
20. 9:13	Malachi 1:2, 3	Jacob I love, Esau I hated
21. 9:15	Exodus 33:19	God's mercy on us
22. 9:17	Exodus 9:16	Pharaoh raised up for God's purpose
23. 9:25	Hosea 2:23	Gentiles called God's people
24. 9:26	Hosea 1:10	Gentiles called not God's people

25.	9:17-28	Isaiah 10:22, 23	Only the remnant will be saved
26.	9:29	Isaiah 1:9	God's provision for descendants
27.	9:33	Isaiah 28:16	Jesus is a stumbling-block
28.	10:5	Leviticus 18:5	Living by the law
29.	10:7-8	Deuteronomy 30:12, 13	Who will ascend into heaven?
30.	10:8	Deuteronomy 30:14	God's word is near you
31.	10:11	Isaiah 28:16	Never being put to shame
32.	10:13	Joel 2:32	Calling on the name of the Lord
33.	10:15	Isaiah 52:7	The feet of those who bring good news
34.	10:16	Isaiah 53:1	Accepting the good news
35.	10:18	Psalm 19:4	Hearing the good news
36.	10:19	Deuteronomy 32:21	Being made envious
37.	10:20	Isaiah 65:1	God is found by those who seek him
38.	10:21	Isaiah 65:2	God holds his hands out
39.	11:31	Kings 19:10, 14	Prophets killed
40.	11:41	Kings 19:18	Prophets God reserved from himself
41.	11:8	Isaiah 29:10	A spirit of stupor
42.	11:9,10	Psalm 69:22, 23	A snare and a stumbling-block
43.	11:26,27	Isaiah 59:20, 21	The deliverer from Zion
44.	11:34	Isaiah 40:13	The mind of the Lord
45.	12:19	Deuteronomy 32:35	Revenge belongs to God
46.	12:20	Proverbs 25:21, 22	Feed your enemy
47.	13:9	Exodus 20:13-17	Commandments
48.	14:11	Isaiah 45:23	Every knee will bow
49.	15:3	Psalm 69:9	Insults fall on Christ
50.	15:9	Psalm 18:49	God's mercy among the Gentiles
51.	15:10	Deuteronomy 32:43	Gentiles and Jews rejoice together
52.	15:11	Psalm 117:1	Gentiles sing the Lord's praises
53.	15:12	Isaiah 11:1, 10	The Root of Jesse
54.	15:21	Isaiah 52:15	Christ preached to the non-Jews

1 Corinthians

EIGHT DOS AND EIGHT DON'TS OF CHRISTIAN LOVE

Charity, love

In 1 Corinthians 13, the word "charity" is translated by "love" in many modern versions.

This chapter lists the qualities of love. It is:

- essential
- kind
- humble
- unselfish
- pure
- longsuffering
- hopeful
- supreme

- patient
- generous
- modest
- mild
- holy
- believing
- eternal

VERSES 4-8	
These verses tell us eight things that love does and does not do.	
Love does	*Love does not*
1. Suffer long, 4	Envy, 4
2. Is kind, 4	Vaunt himself, 4
3. Rejoices in truth, 6	Puff himself up, 4
4. Bear all things, 7	Behave unseemly, 5
5. Believes all things, 7	Seek his own, 5
6. Hopes all things, 7	Provoke easily, 5
7. Endures all things, 7	Think evil, 5
8. Never fails, 8	Rejoice at iniquity, 6

"I" for "love"

If you put in the pronoun "I" for "charity" in 1 Corinthians 13:4-8, see how it reads.

Charity suffereth long, and is kind; charity envieth not; charity vaunteth not itself, is not puffed up,

Doth not behave itself unseemly, seeketh not her own, is not easily provoked, thinketh no evil;

Rejoiceth not in iniquity, but rejoiceth in the truth;

Beareth all things, believeth all things, hopeth all things, endureth all things.

Charity never faileth: but whether there be prophecies, they shall fail; whether there be tongues, they shall cease; whether there be knowledge, it shall vanish away. *1 Corinthians 13:4-8 KJV*

2 Corinthians
TEN EXAMPLES OF PAUL TO FOLLOW

The example of Paul

In 1 Corinthians 11:1 Paul writes, "Follow my example, as I follow the example of Christ." In Paul's second letter to the Corinthians there are at least ten ways in which Paul's example should be followed.

Paul's attitude

1. Paul found God's grace to be sufficient for him:
   2 Corinthians 12:9
2. Paul found that God's power was made perfect in his own weakness:
   2 Corinthians 12:9
3. Paul was able to gladly boast about his weaknesses: 2 Corinthians 12:9
4. Paul was able to delight in persecutions and difficulties:
   2 Corinthians 12:10
5. Despite the pressure he was under, Paul was never crushed:
   2 Corinthians 4:8
6. Despite the pressure he was under, Paul was never in despair:
   2 Corinthians 4:8
7. Despite persecution, Paul knew that God never abandoned him:
   2 Corinthians 4:9
8. Paul was prepared to be a martyr:
   2 Corinthians 4:11
9. Paul longed for Jesus' life to be revealed in his body:
   2 Corinthians 4:11
10. Paul longed for Christ's power to rest on him and on all his work:
    2 Corinthians 12:9

Paul "boasts" about the suffering he endured

Are they ministers of Christ? (I speak as a fool) I am more; in labors more abundant, in stripes above measure, in prisons more frequent, in deaths oft.

Of the Jews five times received I forty stripes save one.

Thrice was I beaten with rods, once was I stoned, thrice I suffered shipwreck, a night and a day I have been in the deep;

In journeyings often, in perils of waters, in perils of robbers, in perils by mine own countrymen, in perils by the heathen, in perils in the city, in perils in the wilderness, in perils in the sea, in perils among false brethren; In weariness and painfulness, in watchings often, in hunger and thirst, in fastings often, in cold and nakedness…

In Damascus the governor under Aretas the king kept the city of the Damascenes with a garrison, desirous to apprehend me:

And through a window in a basket was I let down by the wall, and escaped his hands.

2 Corinthians 11:23-27, 32, 33 KJV

Galatians
17 CONTRASTS

LAW AND GRACE		
The initial statement	*Contrasted with*	*Reference in Galatians*
1. We are in sin	God delivers us from sin	1:4
2. A different gospel	The gospel of Christ	1:6-9
3. Seeking human approval	Seeking God's approval	1:10
4. Human reasoning	Christ's revelation	1:11–2:14
5. Observing the law	Faith in Jesus Christ	2:15-20
6. The law	The grace of God	2:21
7. Human effort	The Spirit	3:1-5
8. Under God's curse	God's righteousness	3:6-16
9. The law's fatal flaw	Salvation through faith in Jesus	3:19-22
10. A hopeless situation	Living with God's promise	3:23-29
11. A slave	A child of God	4:1-7
12. The old covenant	The new covenant	4:10-31
13. Falling from grace	Advancing in grace	5:1-16
14. Living in sinful human nature	Walking in the Spirit	5:17-18
15. Acts of the sinful nature	The fruit of the Spirit	5:19–6:6
16. Discouragement	Encouragement	6:7-10
17. Boasting in the world	Boasting in the cross	6:14

Ephesians
23 SPIRITUAL BLESSINGS

Spiritual blessings in Christ

Paul starts his letter to the Ephesians by writing about the blessings all Christians have been endowed with: See 1:3. There are dozens of these spiritual blessings mentioned in this letter. See: 1:4; 1:5; 1:7; 1:13; 2:5; 2:6; 2:8, 9; 2:10; 2:19; 3:12; 3:16; 3:20; 4:4; 4:7; 4:11-16; 4:23, 24; 5:2; 5:8; 6:11-16.

Philippians

18 WAYS TO LIVE THE CHRISTIAN LIFE

MAKING PROGRESS

Paul's passion was that Christians should grow to become mature in Christ. Philippians 4:4-13 sets out 18 ways in which this is to be achieved.

Topic	Reference in Philippians 4
1. Rejoice always	4
2. Be gentle towards everyone	5
3. Remember the Lord is near	5
4. Have no anxiety	6
5. Prayer about everything	6
6. Give thanks about everything	6
7. Experience God's peace	7
8. Think about what is true	8
9. Think about what is noble ·	8
10. Think about what is right	8
11. Think about what is pure	8
12. Think about what is lovely	8
13. Think about what is admirable	8
14. Think about what is excellent	8
15. Think about what is praiseworthy	8
16. Copy good examples	9
17. Show your concern for others	10
18. Be content in all circumstances	11, 12

Colossians

12 RESULTS FROM BEING RISEN WITH JESUS

THE NEW SELF

One of the apostle Paul's definitions of a Christian was anyone who "has been raised with Christ." In his letter to the Colossians Paul touches on 12 things that should be evident in any Christian.

Topic	Reference in Colossians
1. Set your hearts on things above	3:1
2. Set your minds on things above	3:2
3. Put to death your earthly nature a. Sexual immorality b. Impurity d. Evil desires c. Lust e. Greed	3:3-7
4. Be rid of worldly habits a. Anger d. Slander b. Rage e. Filthy language c. Malice f. Lying	3:8, 9
5. Put on the new self a. Compassion f. Bearing with b. Kindness each other c. Humility g. Forgiving each d. Gentleness other e. Patience h. Love	3:10-15
6. Christ's word living in you	3:16
7. Do everything in Jesus' name	3:17
8. Be obedient	3:22
9. Devote yourself to prayer	4:2
10. Be wise	4:5
11. Speak with much grace	4:6
12. Speak with a little salt	4:7

1 Thessalonians

13 GOOD POINTS ABOUT THE CHRISTIANS OF THESSALONICA

This letter, probably the first one Paul wrote to any church, shows that in many ways the Christians at Thessalonica were a model church. The believers at Thessalonica:

1. Welcomed the message, 1:6
2. Imitated the Lord, 1:6
3. Imitated good Christian leaders, 1:6
4. Had the joy of the Holy Spirit, 1:6
5. Became a model to other believers, 1:7
6. Turned from idols, 1:9
7. Turned to God, 1:9
8. They served God, 1:9
9. Were waiting for Jesus' second coming, 1:10
10. Were rescued from the coming wrath, 1:10
11. Suffered persecution, 3:3
12. Had faith and love, 3:6
13. Stood firm in the Lord, 3:8

2 Thessalonians

FIVE CHARACTERISTICS OF UNBELIEVERS

Those who are not saved:

1. Do not know God, 1:8
2. Do not obey the gospel of Jesus, 1:8
3. Refuse to love the truth, 2:10
4. Do not believe the truth, 2:12
5. Delight in wickedness, 2:12

In chapter 2, verses 1-12 Paul gives a description of the "man of lawlessness." Paul writes about:

1. His character: he is doomed to destruction, 3
2. His time of appearing: not before "the rebellion occurs", that is, the apostasy of the church and Christians falling way, 3
3. His mission: to oppose and exalt himself against God, 4
4. The way he tries to achieve his mission: he sets himself up in God's temple and proclaims that he is God, 4
5. His methods:
   a. Working hand in glove with Satan, 9
   b. Counterfeit miracles, 9
   c. Counterfeit signs and wonders, 9
   d. Every kind of evil that deceives people, 10
6. His destruction: Jesus will overthrow him, and destroy him by the splendor of his coming, 8

1 Timothy

SEVEN EXHORTATIONS TO EXERCISE FAITH

Paul, the seasoned Christian pastor writes to his spiritual son, Timothy, urging him to exercise faith. Each time he mentions faith he links it to another word or words. Link word/s:

1. To have sincere faith, 1:5 (A good conscience)
2. To hold on to faith, 1:19 (A good conscience)
3. To keep hold of the deep truths of the faith, 3:9 (A clear conscience)
4. To be brought up in the truths of the faith, 4:6 (Good teaching)
5. To set an example to the believers in faith, 4:12 (Love and purity)
6. To pursue faith, 6:11 (Righteousness and godliness)
7. To fight the good fight of faith, 6:11 (Love, endurance and gentleness)

2 Timothy

SEVEN ASPECTS OF SALVATION

1. Salvation is by the power of God, 1:8
2. Salvation comes with a calling to live a holy life, 1:9
3. Salvation is not as a result of anything we may have done, 1:9
4. Salvation is in Christ Jesus, 1:9
5. Salvation has been revealed through the appearing of Jesus, 1:10
6. Salvation comes because Jesus has abolished death, 1:10
7. Salvation results in life and immortality to light, 1:10

Titus

SEVEN RESULTS OF SALVATION

The effect of salvation

In two verses in chapter two of Titus Paul spells out seven results of salvation.

1. Self-controlled lives, 12
2. Upright lives, 12
3. Godly lives, 12

4. Redemption, 14
5. Purity, 14
6. A people who are Christ's very own, 14
7. People who are eager to do what is good, 14

Philemon

SEVEN NOTABLE CHARACTERISTICS ABOUT PAUL

In Paul's only surviving personal letter addressed to an individual, he reveals seven of his own good qualities. Even though he was languishing in prison at the time Paul took the trouble to write this letter to help a runaway slave.

1. Paul does not just describe himself as a prisoner, but as "a prisoner of Christ Jesus," 1.
2. Paul describes his friend Philemon as a "fellow-worker," which implies that Paul himself was a worker for Christ, 1.
3. In the same way Paul goes on to describe Archippus as a "fellow-soldier," 2.
4. Paul touches on the point that he always openly shows his gratitude to God: "I always thank my God...," 4.
5. Paul reveals himself to be a man of prayer: "I remember you in my prayers," 4.
6. Paul shows himself to be Philemon's spiritual father when he appeals to him as "my son," 10.
7. Paul mentions again that Philemon's spiritual life is due to Paul, and so shows himself to be a soul-winner, 19.

Hebrews

TEN OLD TESTAMENT EXAMPLES OF FAITH

Hebrews chapter 11 has been called the Westminster Abbey of the Bible, as it gives "epitaphs" about the faith of so many godly men from the Old Testament.

Hebrews 11

Abel

By faith Abel offered unto God a more excellent sacrifice than Cain, by which he obtained witness that he was righteous, God testifying of his gifts: and by it he being dead yet speaketh.

Enoch

By faith Enoch was translated that he should not see death; and was not found, because God had translated him: for before his translation he had this testimony, that he pleased God.

But without faith it is impossible to please him: for he that cometh to God must believe that he is, and that he is a rewarder of them that diligently seek him.

Noah

By faith Noah, being warned of God of things not seen as yet, moved with fear, prepared an ark to the saving of his house; by the which he condemned the world, and became heir of the righteousness which is by faith.

Abraham

By faith Abraham, when he was called to go out into a place which he should after receive for an inheritance, obeyed; and he went out, not knowing whither he went.

By faith he sojourned in the land of promise, as in a strange country, dwelling in tabernacles with Isaac and Jacob, the heirs with him of the same promise:

For he looked for a city which hath foundations, whose builder and maker is God.

Sara

Through faith also Sara herself received strength to conceive seed, and was delivered of a child when she was past age, because she judged him faithful who had promised.

Therefore sprang there even of one, and him as good as dead, so many as the stars of the sky in multitude, and as the sand which is by the sea shore innumerable.

These all died in faith, not having received the promises, but having seen them afar off, and were persuaded of them, and embraced them, and confessed that they were strangers and pilgrims on the earth.

For they that say such things declare plainly that they seek a country.

And truly, if they had been mindful of that country from whence they came out, they might have had opportunity to have returned.

But now they desire a better country, that is, an heavenly: wherefore God is not ashamed to be called their God: for he hath prepared for them a city.

By faith Abraham, when he was tried, offered up Isaac: and he that had received the promises offered up his only begotten son,

Of whom it was said, That in Isaac shall thy seed be called:

Accounting that God was able to raise him up, even from the dead; from whence also he received him in a figure.

Isaac

By faith Isaac blessed Jacob and Esau concerning things to come.

Jacob

By faith Jacob, when he was a dying, blessed both the sons of Joseph; and worshiped, leaning upon the top of his staff.

Joseph

By faith Joseph, when he died, made mention of the departing of the children of Israel; and gave commandment concerning his bones.

Moses

By faith Moses, when he was born, was hid three months of his parents, because they saw he was a proper child; and they were not afraid of the king's commandment.

By faith Moses, when he was come to years, refused to be called the son of Pharaoh's daughter;

Choosing rather to suffer affliction with the people of God, than to enjoy the pleasures of sin for a season;

Esteeming the reproach of Christ greater riches than the treasures in Egypt: for he had respect unto the recompence of the reward.

By faith he forsook Egypt, not fearing the wrath of the king: for he endured, as seeing him who is invisible.

Through faith he kept the passover, and the sprinkling of blood, lest he that destroyed the firstborn should touch them.

By faith they passed through the Red sea as by dry land: which the Egyptians assaying to do were drowned.

By faith the walls of Jericho fell down, after they were compassed about seven days.

Rahab

By faith the harlot Rahab perished not with them that believed not, when she had received the spies with peace.

And what shall I more say? for the time would fail me to tell of Gedeon, and of Barak, and of Samson, and of Jephthae; of David also, and Samuel, and of the prophets:

Who through faith subdued kingdoms, wrought righteousness, obtained promises, stopped the mouths of lions.

Quenched the violence of fire, escaped

the edge of the sword, out of weakness were made strong, waxed valiant in fight, turned to flight the armies of the aliens.

Women received their dead raised to life again: and others were tortured, not accepting deliverance; that they might obtain a better resurrection:

And others had trial of cruel mockings and scourgings, yea, moreover of bonds and imprisonment:

They were stoned, they were sawn asunder, were tempted, were slain with the sword: they wandered about in sheepskins and goatskins; being destitute, afflicted, tormented;

(Of whom the world was not worthy:) they wandered in deserts, and in mountains, and in dens and caves of the earth.

And these all, having obtained a good report through faith, received not the promise:

God having provided some better thing for us, that they without us should not be made perfect. *Hebrews 11:4-40, KJV*

13 TYPES OF FAITH FROM HEBREWS 11		
Person and verse	*Type of faith*	*Illustrating*
Abel, 4	Justifying faith	Worship
Enoch, 5	Sanctifying faith	Walk
Noah, 7	Separating faith	Witness
Abraham, 8	Obedient faith	Trust
Sarah, 11	Strengthening faith	Productiveness
Isaac, 20	Patient faith	Overcoming sin
Jacob, 21	Suffering faith	Overcoming human will
Joseph, 22	Hopeful faith	Waiting
Moses, 23-27	Enduring faith	Being given over to God
Israel, 29	Victorious faith	Joy
Israel, 30	Walking faith	Good deeds
Rahab, 31	Saving faith	Peace
Saints, 32-40	Living faith	Reward

James

24 ANSWERS

DOWN-TO-EARTH		
James is the most practical and down-to-earth letter in the New Testament. It gives answers to the following questions.		
Question	**Answer**	**Relevant verse/s in James**
1. What to do when in trials?	Consider it pure joy	1:2
2. What to do when faith is tested?	Have perseverance	1:3
3. How can I find wisdom?	Ask God for it	1:5
4. How should I ask for wisdom?	By believing and not doubting	1:6
5. What happens if I endure trials?	You will be rewarded with the crown of life	1:12
6. Does God tempt?	No	1:13
7. How am I tempted?	By one's own evil desire	1:14
8. How can I overcome temptation?	Humbly accept the word	1:21
9. How can I be blessed?	By obeying the word	1:22-25
10. What kind of religion does God accept?	Caring for needy people	1:26, 27
11. What is the test for Christian love?	Respecting everyone	2:1-13
12. Is it enough to just have faith?	Faith without action is dead	2:14-26
13. What is the test for a fruitful life?	Controlling one's tongue	3:1-18
14. Why aren't my prayers answered?	Because you ask in the wrong way	4:2, 3
15. Can I have friendship with the world?	No	4:4
16. How can I receive more grace?	By being humble	4:6, 10
17. How can I win over the devil?	By resisting him and submitting to God	4:7, 8
18. What is my life?	A vanishing mist	4:14
19. How long will my life last?	A little while before it vanishes	4:14
20. Is it okey to make my own plans?	Only if it is the Lord's will	4:15
21. How should I live in the light of Christ's coming?	Patiently	5:7, 8
22. Does it matter if I grumble?	Yes, for you should not grumble	5:9
23. How can I face suffering?	Like Job who persevered	5:10, 11
24. How do I face trouble?	With prayer	5:13

1 Peter

NINE FACETS OF THE CHRISTIAN LIFE

1. The Christian life is salvation, 1:18, 19
2. The Christian life is growth, 2:2
3. The Christian life is offering spiritual sacrifices, 2:5
4. The Christian life is being God's chosen people, 2:9a
5. The Christian life is witnessing, 2:9b
6. The Christian life is living as God's servant, 2:16
7. The Christian life involves suffering, 4:12, 13, 19
8. The Christian life involves fighting Satan, 5:6-9
9. The Christian life is being strong and firm in God, 5:10

1 Peter 5:6-9

Humble yourselves therefore under the mighty hand of God, that he may exalt you in due time:
Casting all your care upon him; for he careth for you.
Be sober, be vigilant; because your adversary the devil, as a roaring lion, walketh about, seeking whom he may devour:
Whom resist stedfast in the faith, knowing that the same afflictions are accomplished in your brethren that are in the world. *1 Peter 5:6-9, KJV*

2 Peter

SIX RESULTS FROM GROWING IN GRACE AND KNOWLEDGE OF GOD

Peter's conclusion

Peter ends his second letter with this instruction: "But grow in the grace and knowledge of our Lord and Savior Jesus Christ. To him be glory both now and forever! Amen." *2 Peter 3:18*

The results of grace and knowledge

1. Grace and peace, 1:2
2. All we need for life and godliness, 1:3a
3. We are called by God's own glory and goodness, 1:3b
4. We have God's very great and precious promises, 1:4a
5. We participate in God's divine nature, 1:4b
6. We escape from corruption in the world, 1:4c

1 John

23 COMPARISONS BETWEEN 1 JOHN AND JOHN'S GOSPEL

LINKED THEMES		
John's 1st letter	Similar word, expression, or theme	John's Gospel
1:1	The word	1:1
1:2	Christ manifested	1:14
1:4	Complete joy	15:11
1:5	Light	1:7-9
2:5	Keeping God's word	14:23
2:6, 28	Abiding in Jesus	15:4, 7
2:8a	New commandment	13:34a
2:8b	Light in darkness	1:5
2:10	Nothing to make us stumble	11:10
2:13	Knowing God	17:3

3:1	Children of God	1:12
3:2	Seeing God	17:24
3:8	Satan's deeds	8:44
3:11	Love each other	13:34b
3:13	Being hated by the world	17:14
4:9	One and only Son sent	3:16
4:12	No one has ever seen God	1:18
5:1	Born of God	1:13
5:12	Has the Son	3:36
5:13	I write these things	20:31
5:14	Ask anything	14:13, 14
5:20	The true God	17:2-3
5:20	Eternal life	17:3

2 John

FOUR ATTITUDES A CHRISTIAN SHOULD HAVE TOWARDS TRUTH

1. Walk in truth, verse 4
2. Love the truth, verse 6

3. Abide in truth, verse 9
4. Welcome no falsehood, verses 9-11

3 John

EIGHT WAYS TO SPREAD THE TRUTH

1. By testifying to the truth, verse 3
2. By walking in the truth, verse 3
3. By giving hospitality to traveling Christians, verses 5, 6
4. By working together with fellow Christians, verse 8

5. By exposing malicious gossip, verses 9, 10
6. By resisting evil, verse 11
7. By imitating good, verse 11
8. By communicating with fellow Christians, verse 13

Jude

SIX WAYS TO STRENGTHEN YOUR CHRISTIAN LIFE

SIX "SECRETS" OF THE CHRISTIAN LIFE		
Jude writes his letter to warn Christians against apostasy. He suggests six ways for Christians to strengthen their lives.		
Topic	*Verse in Jude*	*Similar verse elsewhere in NT*
1. By building themselves up in the faith	20	Romans 10:17
2. By praying in the Holy Spirit	20	1 Thessalonians 5:17
3. By keeping themselves in God's love	21	Romans 12:9
4. Be alert to Christ's return	21	Luke 19:13
5. Have mercy on those who doubt	22-23	Matthew 9:36-39
6. Rely on Christ	24	Philippians 4:13

Jude 20-25

But ye, beloved, building up yourselves on your most holy faith, praying in the Holy Ghost,

Keep yourselves in the love of God, looking for the mercy of our Lord Jesus Christ unto eternal life.

And of some have compassion, making a difference:

And others save with fear, pulling them out of the fire; hating even the garment spotted by the flesh.

Now unto him that is able to keep you from falling, and to present you faultless before the presence of his glory with exceeding joy,

To the only wise God our Savior, be glory and majesty, dominion and power, both now and ever. Amen. *Jude 20-25, KJV*

WHAT LEADS TO APOSTASY?	
Jude gives six examples from the Old Testament.	
The person and how they failed	*Verse in Jude*
1. The example of Israel and their unbelief	5
2. The example of the angels and their rebellion	6
3. The example of Sodom and Gomorrah and their immorality	7
4. The example of Cain and his self-will	11
5. The example of Balaam and his covetousness	11
6. The example of Korah and his rejection of God	11

Revelation

LINKS BETWEEN THE BOOK OF REVELATION AND OTHER BIBLE BOOKS

THE BOOK OF REVELATION COMPARED WITH OTHER BIBLE BOOKS		
Verses from other Bible books	*Common themes*	*Verses in Revelation*
"He will strike your head" Genesis 3:15.	1. Jesus Christ	"The revelation of Jesus Christ" 1:1. See 1:13-18
"...I will build my church, and the gates of Hades will not overcome it" Matthew 16:18.	2. God's persevering church	"You have persevered and endured hardship for my name" 2:3.
"...imitate those who through faith and patience inherit what has been promised" Hebrews 6:12.	3. A call to be faithful	"This calls for patient endurance and faithfulness on the part of the saints" 13:10.
"Just as man is destined to die once, and after that to face judgment..." Hebrews 9:27.	4. God's judgment	"And I saw the dead, great and small, standing before the throne,...The dead were judged..." 20:12.
"...the new heavens and the new earth that I make will endure..." Isaiah 66:22.	5. A new heaven and a new earth	"...a new heaven and a new earth..." 21:1.

GENESIS AND REVELATION	
There are many similar themes in the first book and the last book of the Bible.	
Genesis	*Revelation*
1. Creation of the sun	No need for the sun
2. Satan appears to be victorious	Satan is seen to be defeated
3. Sin enters the world	Sin is banished
4. Humankind is defeated	Humankind is victorious
5. Humankind hides from God	Humankind is invited back into God's presence
6. Curses are pronounced	There will be no more curses
7. Tears and sorrow	No more crying
8. The garden is cursed	The city is glorified
9. The fruit of the tree of life is forbidden	The fruit from the tree of life is eaten
10. Paradise is lost	Paradise is regained
11. Death enters the world	There will be no more death

Firsts and lasts

The first book: The first book of the Bible places humankind in a garden.
The last book: The last book of the Bible places humankind in a city, the new Jerusalem. *Revelation 21:10, 23-27*

The first book: The first book of the Bible tells how humankind lost paradise, in Genesis 3.
The last book: The last book of the Bible tells how humankind regained paradise, in Revelation 21–22.

The first book: The first book of the Bible concludes with death and a coffin, see Genesis 50:56.
The last book: The last book of the Bible ends with resurrection and life, see Revelation 20:5; 22:14.

The last book: The last book of the Old Testament concludes with a curse, see Malachi 4:6.

The last book of the New Testament ends with a blessing.

"The grace of the Lord Jesus be with God's people." *Revelation 22:21*

Seven

The book of Revelation is full of symbols. The most frequently occurring symbol is the number seven. It stands for perfection and completeness. Six stands for humankind. This book was written during a time when Christians were being fiercely persecuted. The book of Revelation was written to encourage these Christians with the message that the world was not out of control and that ultimately God would judge the world.

So many sevens

1. Seven churches, 1:4
2. Seven spirits, 1:4
3. Seven lampstands, 1:12
4. Seven stars, 1:16
5. Seven seals, 5:1
6. Seven horns, 5:6
7. Seven angels, 8:2
8. Seven trumpets, 8:2
9. Seven thunders, 10:3
10. Seven heads, 12:3
11. Seven last plagues, 15:1
12. Seven golden bowls, 15:7
13. Seven kings, 17:10

Seven beatitudes in Revelation

1. "Blessed is the one who reads the words of this prophecy" 1:3.
2. "Blessed are the dead who die in the Lord from now on" 14:13.
3. "Blessed is he who stays awake [looking for Christ's coming]" 16:15.
4. "Blessed are those who are invited to the wedding supper of the Lamb" 19:9.
5. "Blessed and holy are those who have part in the first resurrection" 20:6.
6. "Blessed is he who keeps the words of the prophecy of this book" 22:7.
7. "Blessed are those who wash their robes" 22:14.

5 KEY EVENTS AND LISTS OF IMPORTANT TOPICS

Introduction

This chapter includes sections about the history of both the Old and New Testaments. History sometimes gets a bad press. It's been said that history is something that the English never remember, the Irish never forget and the Americans never had. Henry Ford famously said, "All history is bunk." But our understanding of what God is saying in the Bible is helped if we know something about the history of God's people. Isaiah's message to King Hezekiah, "In repentance and rest is your salvation" (Isaiah 30:15) gains in power when we know the terrible danger facing Israel at the time.

Our understanding of the New Testament is helped if we know a little about each of the religious groups mentioned in the Gospels. Unlike the Pharisees, for example, the Sadducees did not believe in life after death. This sheds light on an incident recorded in Acts 23 when Paul was hauled up in front of the Jewish court, the Sanhedrin. Paul successfully divided his opponents with a single sentence. "I stand on trial because of my hope in the resurrection of the dead" (Acts 23:6). At once the Pharisees and Sadducees were at each other's throats in intense theological debate. The result was that the Pharisees supported Paul, affirming: "We find nothing wrong with this man" (Acts 23:9).

In our reading of the Bible, we may have stumbled over phrases like "the month of Abib," or, "the spring rains," and have wondered how this links up with the seasons and festivals that we have in the world of the twenty-first century. This chapter explains such topics.

Time-lines
THE OLD TESTAMENT

FROM ADAM TO JESUS	
THE BEGINNINGS	
Unknown	Creation of universe
Unknown	Creation of Adam and Eve
Unknown	The flood and Noah's ark
THE ANCESTORS OF THE ISRAELITES	
2166	Birth of Abram
2116	Abram migrates to Haran
2091	Abram enters Canaan
2056	Sodom and Gomorrah destroyed
2066	Isaac is born
2026	Isaac marries Rebekah
1883	Joseph viceroy in Egypt
THE ISRAELITES IN EGYPT	
1527	Birth of Moses
1486	Moses flees to Midian
1446	Exodus from Egypt
1445	Law given at Mount Sinai
1406	Death of Moses
CONQUEST AND SETTLEMENT OF CANAAN	
1406	Fall of Jericho
1406–1382	Conquest of Canaan
1400	Land divided among 12 tribes
1375	Joshua dies. See *The judges of Israel*, p 127
THE UNITED ISRAELITE KINGDOM	
1063	Samuel judge and prophet
1043	Saul becomes Israel's first king
1040	Birth of David
1035	Philistines capture ark
1010	Death of Saul and Jonathan
1010	David made king of Judah
1003	David reigns over all of Israel

1003	David captures Jerusalem
970	Death of David
970	Solomon becomes king
959	King Solomon's temple dedicated
930	Death of Solomon
THE TWO ISRAELITE KINGDOMS	
930	Kingdom divided. See *The kings of Israel and Judah*, p 128
722	Samaria falls to Assyria
587	Judah falls to Babylon See *The prophets of Israel and Judah*, p 130
EXILE AND RETURN	
538	Jews return to Jerusalem under Sheshbazzar (Zerubabel)
516	New temple completed
481	Esther is Queen
458	Ezra returns to Jerusalem
445	Nehemiah returns to Jerusalem
445	Wall of Jerusalem rebuilt
THE TIME BETWEEN THE TESTAMENTS: JEWISH HISTORY	
429	Malachi, the last Old Testament prophet
424–333	Palestine ruled by Persian governor
333	Alexander the Great establishes Greek rule in Palestine
323-166	Descendants of Alexander's generals, the Ptolemies and Seleucids rule Palestine
167	Antiochus IV desecrates the Temple
166-63	Jews revolt under Judas Maccabaeus
63	Roman general, Pompey takes Jerusalem
37–4	Puppet kings, appointed by Rome rule Palestine, like Herod the Great
6/5 BC	Birth of Jesus

Time-lines
THE NEW TESTAMENT

THE EARY CHRISTIANS	
AD 26	Death of John the Baptist
AD 30	Crucifixion of Jesus
AD 34	Conversion of Saul
AD 44	James, the brother of John, martyred
AD 50	Jerusalem council meets
AD 67	Peter and Paul executed in Rome
AD 70	Jerusalem falls to Titus
AD 90	Apostle John exiled to Patmos
AD 100	Apostle John dies

See *The Life of Jesus*, pp 132-134
See *The Life of Paul*, p 135

4004 BC
From the genealogies found in the early chapters of Genesis Bishop Ussher calculated that God created the world in 4004 BC. Today, most Bible scholars do not believe that there is enough information given in the Bible to be certain about any precise dates for any of the events recorded in Genesis 1–11.

They point out that Hebrew genealogies often list important members in a family, but not every person. The dates suggested in this book reflect the best attempts of conservative scholars to solve many of the dating problems which exist.

Chronological problems
There are some problems about dating the events recorded in the Old Testament because of the few cross-references to established dates in secular history before the battle of Qarqar in 853 BC. This does not mean that the events did not happen, but that in common with other ancient civilizations, accurate dates are often impossible to determine. For example, although Egyptian dynasties have many artifacts and written records, their dates remain uncertain.

The New Testament
Some of the events recorded in the New Testament cannot be dated precisely. In New Testament times people often referred to another well-known event, rather than giving a date as we do, when they were recording a particular event. Luke adopts this method when he records the birth of Jesus, and writes, "This was the first census that took place while Quirinius was governor of Syria" (Luke 2:2). Luke uses this same method of dating when he introduces John the Baptist, when he writes, "In the fifteenth year of the reign of Tiberius Caesuar... the word of God came to John son of Zechariah in the desert" (Luke 3:1-2).

Categories of the Mosaic law

1. Criminal law
Crimes against God

- Blasphemy: Leviticus 24:16
- Human sacrifice: Leviticus 29:2-5
- Idolatry: Exodus 22:20;
  Deuteronomy 13:1-18

Crimes of personal injury

- Murder: Exodus 21:12-14;
  Numbers 35:16-34
- Oppression: Exodus 22:21-24

Property-related crimes

- Fraud: Leviticus 6:1-7;
  Deuteronomy 25:13-16
- Theft: Exodus 22:1-3;
  Leviticus 19:35, 36

Sexual crimes

- Adultery: Leviticus 20:10-12;
  Deuteronomy 22:22-24
- Fornication: Deuteronomy 22:13-21
- Homosexuality: Leviticus 20:13
- Incest: Leviticus 20:11-14
- Prostitution: Leviticus 19:29; 21:9

2. Laws concerning the family
Marriage

- Divorce: Deuteronomy 24:1-4
- Husband's responsibilities:
  Numbers 30:6-15
- Wife's rights: Deuteronomy 21:10-14

Children and parents

- Child's responsibility: Exodus 20:12
- Parents' responsibility: Numbers
  18:15, 17; Deuteronomy 6:6, 7

3. Cultic law

- About giving: Deuteronomy 14:22-29
- About the Sabbath: Exodus 20:8-11
- About sacrifice: Leviticus 1–7
- About other religions:
  Deuteronomy 7:13

4. Laws about property rights

- Inheritance: Deuteronomy 21:15-17;
  Numbers 36:1-12

5. Laws about humane treatment
Land and animals

- Crop rotation: Exodus 23:11, 12;
  Leviticus 25:3-7
- Feeding and care: Deuteronomy 25:4;
  Exodus 20:8-11

People

- Elderly: Leviticus 19:32
- Foreigners: Numbers 15:13-16,
  29-31
- Helpless: Exodus 22:21-23
- Poor: Leviticus 25:35-37
- Servants: Leviticus 19:13;
  Deuteronomy 24:14
- Slaves: Exodus 21:2-6;

6 Leadership law

- Qualifications: Deuteronomy 23:1-3
- Prophets: Deuteronomy 18:14-22

7 Military law

- Military service: Numbers 31:3-6;
  Deuteronomy 17:16; 23:9-14
- Exemptions: Deuteronomy 20:5-8;
  24:5

The judges of Israel

JUDGES				
Oppressor	*Years of oppression*	*Judge/Deliverer*	*Reference in Judges*	*Years of peace*
Mesopotamians	8	Othniel	3:7-11	40
Moabites	18	Ehud	3:12-30	80
Philistines	–	Shagmar	3:31	–
Canaanites	20	Deborah, Barak	4:1–5:31	40
Midianites	7	Gideon	6:1–8:32	40
Abimelech	3	Tola, Jair	8:33–10:5	45
Ammonites	18	Jepthah, Ibzan, Elon, Abdon	10:6–12:15	6, 7 10, 8
Philistines	40	Samson	13:1–16:31	20

The judges

The judges of the Old Testament were civil and military leaders during a time when the Israelites lived under a loose confederacy. 13 judges are mentioned in the book of Judges, and four more, Eli, Samuel, Joel, and Abijah, in 1 Samuel. The judges succeeded in freeing Israel from their different oppressors. So the first judge, Othniel led Israel to freedom from Mesopotamian oppressors, and Samson did the same, releasing Israel from the Philistines.

The book of Judges

The book of Judges covers the history of the Israelites between their conquest of Canaan and the time they appointed their first kings.

The book of Judges follows seven similar cycles, which have been called "sin" cycles.

Sin cycles

1. Sin - The Israelites turn from God
2. Oppression - The Israelites are oppressed by a foreign enemy
3. Repentance - The Israelites turn back to God
4. Deliverance - God raises up a "judge" as a deliverer for the Israelites
5. Peace - The Israelites enjoy a time of peace

The kings of Israel and Judah

THE UNITED KINGDOM SPLITS INTO TWO KINGDOMS		
Kingdom	Number of years	BC Dates
The united kingdom	112 years	1043–931
The northern kingdom of Israel	209 years	931–722
The southern kingdom of Judah	345 years	931–586

THE KINGS OF ISRAEL			
Name of king	Bible reference	Length of reign	BC Dates
Jeroboam I	1 Kings 12:25–14:20	22 years	930–909
Nadab	1 Kings 15:25-31	2 years	909–908
Baasha	1 Kings 15:32–16:7	24 years	908–886
Elah	1 Kings 16:8-14	2 years	886–885
Zimri	1 Kings 16:15-20	7 days	885
Tibni	1 Kings 16:21, 22	overlaps with Omri	885–880
Omri	1 Kings 16:23-28	12 years	880–874
Ahab	1 Kings 16:29–22:40	22 years	874–853
Ahaziah	1 Kings 22:51–2 Kings 1:18	2 years	853–852
Joram	2 Kings 1:17	12 years	852–841
Jehu	2 Kings 9:30–10:36	28 years	841–814
Jehoahaz	2 Kings 13:1-9	17 years	814–798
Jehoash	2 Kings 13:10-25	16 years	798–782
Jeroboam II	2 Kings 14:23-29	41 years	793–753
Zechariah	2 Kings 15:8-12	6 months	753
Shallum	2 Kings 15:13-15	1 month	752
Menahem	2 Kings 15:16-22	10 years	752–742
Pekahiah	2 Kings 15:23-26	2 years	742–740
Pekah	2 Kings 15:27-31	20 years	752–732
Hoshea	2 Kings 15:30–17:6	9 years	732–722

THE KINGS OF JUDAH			
Name of king	Bible reference	Length of reign	BC Dates
Rehoboam	1 Kings 11:42–14:31	17 years	930–913
Abijah	1 Kings 14:31–15:8	3 years	913–910
Asa	1 King 15:8-24	41 years	910–869
Jehoshaphat	1 Kings 22:41-50	25 years	872–848
Jehoram	2 Kings 8:16-24	8 years	848–841
Ahaziah	2 Kings 8:24–9:29	1 years	841
Athaliah (Queen)	2 Kings 11:1-20	7 years	841–835
Joash	2 Kings 12	40 years	835–796
Amaziah	2 Kings 14:1-22	29 years	796–767
Azariah	2 Kings 15:1-7	overlap with Amaziah	792–740
Jotham	2 Kings 15:32-38	overlap with Azariah	750–732
Ahaz	2 Kings 16:1-20	16 years	732–715
Hezekiah	2 Kings 18:1–20:21	29 years	715–686
Manasseh	2 Kings 21:1-18	overlap with Hezekiah	697–642
Amon	2 Kings 21:19-26	2 years	642–640
Josiah	2 Kings 21:1–23:30	31 years	640–609
Jehoahaz	2 Kings 23:31-33	3 months	609
Jehoiakim	2 Kings 23:34–24:5	11 years	609–598
Jehoiachin	2 Kings 24:6-16	3 months	598–597
Zedekiah	2 Kings 24:17–25:30	11 years	597–586

Kings of Judah in the time of Jeremiah

Manasseh - Jeremiah was born when this wicked tyrant ruled.

Amon - Like his father Manasseh Amon worshiped idols.

Josiah - Josiah, a godly king, began his reforms in 627. He discovered the Book of the law and carried out its instructions.

Jehoahaz - Jehoahaz only reigned for three months before he was taken off to Egypt.

Jehoiakim - Jehoiakim was a wicked king who indulged in idolatry.

Jehoiachin - Jehoiachin only reigned for three months before he was exiled in Babylon.

Zedekiah - Zedekiah was king of Judah when Jerusalem was sacked in 586 and the temporary end of the Davidic dynasty occurred. His rebellion spelled the doom of Judah. See 2 Chronicles 36:11-21.

The prophets of Israel and Judah

THE PROPHETS OF ISRAEL AND JUDAH			
Name	*Date*	*Spoken to*	*World ruler*
Isaiah	c. 740–680	Pre-exile: Judah	Assyria
Jeremiah	c. 627–580	Pre-exile: Judah	Assyria and Babylonia
Ezekiel	c. 593–571	Exile: Exiles in Babylon	Babylonia
Daniel	c. 605–535	Exile: Exiles in Babylonia	Babylonia and Medo-Persia
Hosea	c. 755–715	Pre-exile: Israel	Assyria
Joel	c. 835	Pre-exile: Judah	Assyria
Amos	c. 760–753	Pre-exile: Israel	Assyria
Obadiah	c. 848–841	Pre-exile: Edom	Assyria
Jonah	c. 782–753	Pre-exile: Assyria	Assyria
Micah	c. 735–700	Pre-exile: Judah	Assyria
Nahum	c. 664–654	Pre-exile: Assyria	Assyria
Habakkuk	c. 609–605	Pre-exile: Judah	Babylonia
Zephaniah	c. 632–628	Pre-exile: Judah	Assyria
Haggai	c. 520	Post-exile: Returned Jews in Jerusalem from Babylonia	Medo-Persia
Zechariah	c. 520–480	Post-exile: Returned Jews in Jerusalem from Babylonia	Medo-Persia
Malachi	c. 432–424	Post-exile: Returned Jews in Jerusalem from Babylonia	Medo-Persia

THE PROPHETS OF ISRAEL AND JUDAH

Bible context	OT reference to prophet	Theme
2 Kings 15:1–20:21; 2 Chronicles 26:16–32:33 2 Kings 19–20; 2 Chronicles 26:22; 32:20, 32	Isaiah	Salvation is from the Lord
2 Kings 22:3–25:30; 2 Chronicles 34:1–36:21; 2 Chronicles 35:25; 36:12,21ff; Ezra 1:1; Daniel 9:2	Jeremiah	Warning about God's impending judgment
2 Kings 24:8–25:30; 2 Chronicles 36:9-21; Ezekiel 1:3; 24:24		The glory of the Lord
2 Kings 23:34–25:30; 2 Chronicles 36:4-23; Ezekiel 14:14, 20; 28:3	Daniel	God's sovereignty over individuals and nations
2 Kings 14:23–18:12; Hosea 1:1, 2		God's love
2 Kings 12:1-21; 2 Chronicles 24:1-27; Joel 1:1		The day of the Lord
2 Kings 14:23–15:7; Amos 1:1; 7:8-14; 8:2		Judgment on Israel
2 Kings 8:16-24; 2 Chronicles 21:1-20; Obadiah 1		Judgment on Edom
2 Kings 13:10-25; 14:23-29; 2 Kings 14:25	Jonah	Salvation for the Gentiles
2 Kings 15:32–19:37; 2 Chronicles 27:1–32:23; Micah 1:1; Jeremiah 26:18		Corruption of Judah and God's justice
2 Kings 21:1-18; 2 Chronicles 33:1-20; Nahum 1:1		Destruction of Nineveh
2 Kings 23:31–24:7; 2 Chronicles 36:1-8; Habakkuk 1:1; 3:1		The just will live by faith
2 Kings 22:1, 2; 2 Chronicles 34:1-7; Zephaniah 1:1		The day of the Lord will bring judgment and blessing
Ezra 5:1–6:15; Ezra 5:1; 6:14	Haggai	Rebuilding the Jerusalem temple
Ezra 5:1–6:15; Ezra 5:1; 6:14; Nehemiah 12:16; Zechariah 1:1, 7; 7:1, 8		God's future blessing on Israel
Nehemiah 13:1-31; Malachi 1:1		A message to backsliders to return to God

The life of Jesus

7 BC TO AD 28		
Date	*Topic*	*New Testament reference*
BIRTH AND CHILDHOOD		
7 BC	Birth foretold by angel	Luke 1:26-38
6 BC	Birth of Jesus	Luke 2:1-7; Matthew 1:18-25
6 BC	Visit by shepherds	Luke 2:8-17
6 BC	Presentation in temple	Luke 2:22-24
4 BC	Visit by Magi	Matthew 2:1-12
4 BC	Escape to Egypt	Matthew 2:13-15
2 BC	Return to Nazareth	Matthew 2:19-23
AD 6	Visit to temple	Matthew 2:41-50
AD 6–26	Silent years. No recorded events	Luke 2:51-52
YEAR OF INAUGURATION AD 26–27		
AD 26	Baptism of Jesus	Matthew 3:13-17
26	Temptation of Jesus	Matthew 4:1-11
27	Jesus' first miracle, at Cana	John 2:1-11
27	Jesus cleanses the temple	John 2:14-22
27	Jesus' first meeting with Nicodemus	John 3:1-21
27	Jesus talks with the Samaritan woman	John 4:5-42
27	Jesus heals a nobleman's son	John 4:46-54
27	People of Nazareth try to kill Jesus	Luke 4:16-31
YEAR OF POPULARITY AD 27–28		
27	Four fishermen follow Jesus	Matthew 4:18-22
27	Peter's mother-in-law healed	Mark 1:29-34
27	Jesus' first preaching tour through Galilee	Mark 1:35-39
27	Matthew becomes follower of Jesus	Matthew 9:9-13
28	Jesus chooses 12 apostles	Luke 6:12-15
28	Sermon on Mount preached	Matthew 5–7
28	Jesus anointed by a sinful woman	Luke 7:36-50
28	Jesus tells parables about the kingdom	Matthew 13:1-52
28	Jesus calms the storm	Mark 4:35-41
28	Jairus' daughter brought back to life	Luke 8:40-56
28	Jesus sends out the 12 to preach and heal	Mark 6:6-13

Luke and the prayers of Jesus

Each of the four Gospel writers emphasizes different facets of Jesus. One of the things Luke concentrates on is Jesus' prayer life.

Luke records the following ten prayers of Jesus:

1. At Jesus' baptism, 3:21
2. In the desert, 5:16
3. Before appointing the Twelve, 6:12, 13
4. At Caesarea Philippi, 9:18
5. Before his transfiguration, 9:28, 29
6. The Lord's Prayer, 11:1-4
7. His prayer for Peter, 22:31, 32
8. In Gethsemane, 22:41
9. One the cross, 23:24
10. At Emmaus, 24:30

The trials of Jesus

One of the underlying purposes of the evangelists is to present Jesus as an innocent man who was wrongly condemned to death. The evangelists record a total of six trials of Jesus which took place on the Thursday night and Friday morning.

Pilate's verdict was: "I have examined him in your presence and have found no basis for your charges against him. Neither has Herod, for he sent him back to us; as you can see, he has done nothing to deserve death." *Luke 23:14, 15*

Pilate went on to say, "I have found in him no grounds for the death penalty. Therefore I will have him punished and then release him." *Luke 23:22*

YEAR OF OPPOSITION
AD 29
Herod kills John the Baptist, Mark 6:14-29
Jesus feeds 5,000, Mark 6:30-44
Jesus walks on the water, Mark 6:45-52
Jesus withdraws to Tyre and Sidon, Mark 7:24-30
Jesus feeds 4,000, Mark 8:1-9
Peter declares that Jesus is the Son of God, Mark 8:27-30
Jesus foretells his suffering, Mark 8:31-37
Jesus' transfiguration, Mark 9:2-13
Jesus pays his temple tax, Matthew 17:24-27
Jesus goes to the feast of tabernacles, John 7:11-52
Man born blind healed, John 9:1-41
Jesus visits Mary and Martha, Luke 10:38-42
Lazarus is raised from the dead, John 11:1-44
AD 30
Jesus starts his last journey to Jerusalem, Luke 17:11
Little children blessed, Luke 18:15-17
Rich young man and Jesus, Luke 18:18-30
Jesus foretells his death and resurrection, Luke 18:31-34
Jesus heals blind Bartimaeus, Luke 18:35-43
Jesus meets Zacchaeus, Luke 19:1-10
Jesus visits Mary and Martha, John 11:55–12:1

SIX TRIALS			
Trial	*Reference in Gospel*	*Judge*	*Decision*
RELIGIOUS JEWISH TRIALS			
First	John 18:12-14	Annas	No verdict reached
Second	Matthew 26:57-68	Caiaphas	Charged with blasphemy. Death sentence
Third	Matthew 27:1, 2	Sanhedrin	Death sentence
CIVIL ROMAN TRIALS			
Fourth	John 18:28-38	Pilate	Not guilty
Fifth	Luke 23:6-12	Herod	Not guilty
Sixth	John 18:39–19:6	Pilate	Not guilty. Pilate hands Jesus over to the Jews

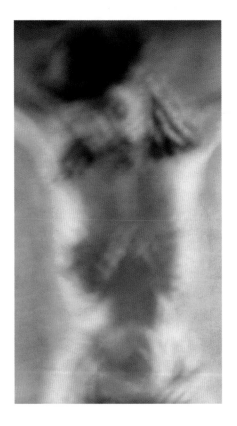

Jesus' last week

- *Sunday* Jesus' triumphal entry into Jerusalem, Mark 11:1-11
- *Monday* Jesus clears the temple of traders, Mark 11:15-18
- *Tuesday* Day of parables and controversy, Mark 11:27–13:37
- *Wednesday* Nothing recorded in the Gospels. Probably day of rest at Bethany.
- *Thursday* The Last Supper Mark, 14:12-28
- *Thursday* Jesus prays and is arrested in Gethsemane, Mark 14:32-52
- *Thursday/Friday* Jesus' false trials, Mark 14:53–15:15
- *Friday* Jesus is crucified, John 19:16–19:37
- *Friday* Jesus' body is laid in Joseph's tomb, John 19:38-42
- *Saturday* Nothing recorded.
- *Sunday* Jesus' resurrection, John 20:1-31

The life of Paul

APOSTLE AND MISSIONARY

EARLY LIFE

5	Birth of Paul. Born in Tarsus, Acts 22:3
15-25	Educated in Judaism, Acts 22:3
35	Witnessed Stephen's martyrdom, Acts 7:58
35	Persecuted Christians, Acts 9:1, 2
35	Conversion near Damascus, Acts 9:3-18
35-38	Staying in Arabia, Galatians 1:17
38	Visits Jerusalem for two weeks, Acts 9:26-29; Galatians 1:18-19
38-43	Preached in Syria and Cilicea, Acts 9:30
39	Taken back to Tarsus, Acts 9:30
39	Brought to Antioch, Acts 11:25, 26
43	Further visit to Jerusalem, Acts 11:27-30

FIRST MISSIONARY TOUR

46-48	First missionary tour, Acts 13:2–14:28
	Evangelism in...
46	Cyprus, Acts 13:4-12
46	Perga, Acts 13:13
46	Pisidian Antioch, Acts 13:14-50
46	Iconium, Acts 13:51–14:5
46	Lystra, Acts 14:6-19
47	Derbe, Acts 14:20
47	Return to Lystra, Iconium, Pisidian Antioch, Acts 14:21-24
47	Perga, Attalia, Acts 14:25
48	Syrian Antioch, Acts 14:26-28
51/52	Appears before Gallio, Acts 18:12-17

SECOND MISSIONARY TOUR

50-52	Second missionary tour, Acts 15:40–18:23
50	Antioch by land through Syria and Cilicia, Acts 15:41
50	Derbe and Lystra, Acts 16:1-5
50	Phrygia and Galatia, Acts 16:6
50	Troas, Samothrace, Neapolis, Philippi, Acts 16:8-40
51	Thessalonica, Acts 17:1-9
51	Berea, Acts 17:10-14
51	Athens, Acts 17:15-34
51	Corinth, Acts 18:1-17
52	Ephesus, Caesarea, Jerusalem, Acts 18:18-22
52	Return to Antioch, Acts 18:22

THIRD MISSIONARY TOUR

53-57	Third missionary tour, Acts 18:23–21:17
53	Galatia and Phrygia, Acts 18:23
53-55	Ephesus, Acts 19:1-41
56	Macedonia and Achaia, Acts 20:1-5
57	Troas, Acts 20:6-12
57	Miletus, Acts 20:13-38
57	Visits Jerusalem, Acts 21:1-17
57	Arrested in Jerusalem, Acts 21:27–22:30

IN PRISON AND DEATH

57-59	In prison at Caesarea, Acts 23:23–26:32
59	Journey, including shipwreck, to Rome, Acts 27
59	Arrives in Rome, Acts 28:16
59-61	First imprisonment in Rome, Acts 28:16-31
62	Release from prison
62-67	Fourth missionary journey, including Crete, Titus 1:5
67	Second imprisonment in Rom, 2 Timothy 4:6-8
67	Trial and execution

New Testament sects and parties: political

"dagger-men" because they always carried daggers and used them whenever they could against the Roman soldiers.

One of Jesus' disciples, Simon, belonged to this Jewish sect, and was known as Simon the Zealot, Acts 1:13. The Zealots looked forward to the time when a messiah would came and rescue them and thought of him as a conquering warrior. They were against paying taxes to their foreign rulers.

They held similar religious beliefs as the Pharisees. Their battle cry was,

"No Lord but Jehovah;
no tax but that of the Temple,
No friend but the Zealots."

They came into existence at the time of Herod the Great but were defeated when the Romans sacked Jerusalem in AD 70, and were wiped out in AD 73 when they took their last stand at Masada.

Herodians

This Jewish sect believed that the best way to support Judaism was to submit to the rule of Rome. They sought to perpetuate the line of Herod so that Israel at least had the semblance of a government of its own, Mark 3:6.

Zealots

The Zealots had the same aim as the Herodians but a completely opposite method by which to attain it. They were freedom fighters and could not abide being under the heel of Rome. They used every opportunity to stir up trouble against the Romans, who called them

Galileans

Galileans believed that the scriptures taught that it was wrong for any foreign power to rule over them, so they always refused to acknowledge the Roman rule in Palestine. As their beliefs were so similar to the Zealots they eventually joined forces with them.

Jesus referred to them once, Luke 13:1, and one Galilean is mentioned by name in Acts 5:37, "Judas the Galilean appeared in the days of the census and led a band of people in revolt. He too was killed, and all his followers were scattered."

New Testament sects and parties: social

Teachers of the law (scribes)

One major part of the work of the teachers of the law was to copy, teach, and explain the law. As they were copyists of scripture they knew the Mosaic law intimately. They often showed in their opposition to Jesus that they were more concerned with the letter of the law than the spirit of the law.

In common with the Pharisees, they believed and kept the oral law, as well as the written law of the scriptures.

- They acted as lawyers and judges and were held in high esteem in Jewish society.
- They interpreted the scriptures, Matthew 2:4.
- They tested Jesus, John 18:3.
- They were offended by Jesus' teaching, Matthew 21:15; Mark 2:6-17.
- Jesus condemned them as hypocrites, Matthew 23:15.
- They tried to have Jesus killed, Matthew 26:3; Luke 23:10.
- They persecuted the early Christians, Acts 4:5, 18, 21; 6:12.

"Watch out for the teachers of the law"

"As he taught, Jesus said, 'Watch out for the teachers of the law. They like to walk around in flowing robes and be greeted in the market-places, and have the most important seats in the synagogues and the places of honor at banquets. They devour widows' houses and for a show make lengthy prayers. Such men will be punished most severely.'" *Mark 12:38-40*

Tax-collectors

Tax-collectors (publicans), who collected taxes in Palestine for the Romans, were understandably hated by the Jews. Their work was viewed as an act of treachery and they were also regarded as being "unclean" because of all their contact with Gentiles (non-Jews). The Jews despised them, Luke 18:11.

- They were often guilty of extortion, Luke 3:13; 19:8.
- The chief tax-collectors were very rich, Luke 19:2.
- They accepted John the Baptist's message and his baptism, Matthew 21:32; Luke 3:12.
- One of Jesus' disciples, Matthew, was a tax-collector when Jesus called him, Mark 2:14.

New Testament sects and parties: religious

Pharisees

History of the Pharisees

During the reign of the Maccabean, John Hyrcanus, 134–104 BC, the opposing parties in Judaism, the Pharisees, Sadducees, and Essenes, were formed. The Pharisees were the successors to the old Jewish party known as the Hasidim ("the pious"). The Pharisees thus became the master interpreters of the oral traditions of the rabbis.

According to Josephus there were about 6,000 Pharisees in Palestine in Jesus' day. Ordinary people stood in awe of the Pharisees. Josephus also noted that when people faced a difficult decision they took more notice of the opinion of the Pharisees than that of the king or high priest.

Unlike the priests, they were laymen, and were a well-known Jewish sect, Acts 15:5, and held the religious power in Palestine throughout Jesus' ministry.

What did the Pharisees believe?

- They wholeheartedly accepted all of the teachings of the Torah. The Pharisees, or, "separated ones" believed that their very detailed descriptions about how to obey the law (their oral tradition) were on a par with the Mosaic law. So the meticulous way in which they kept all the Jewish traditions elevated them into being the only truly righteous Jews in the world. They became rigid and legalistic in their interpretation of the Jewish law.
- They believed in the supernatural. The believed in demons and angels.
- They believed in praying.
- They believed in fasting.
- They believed in tithing, right down to the tiny herbs that grew in their gardens.
- They believed in the resurrection, Acts 23:8, and life after death and taught that righteous people would live again after death, but that the unrepentant would be punished for eternity.

How did the Pharisees live?

- They strictly observed all Mosaic ritual, Acts 26:5.
- They kept the law, Philippians 3:5.
- They kept all their traditions, Mark 7:3, 5-8; Galatians 1:14.
- Outwardly, they led very moral lives, Luke 16:11; 18:9.
- They sought to win converts, Matthew 23:15.

What was wrong with the Pharisees?

- They were self-righteous, Luke 16:15; 18:9.
- They loved to recognized in public, Matthew 23:7.
- They loved to be called by distinguished titles, Matthew 7-10.
- They were cruel persecutors, Acts 9:1, 2.
- They wore special clothes so that

they would be noticed,
Matthew 23:5.
- They had rejected John the Baptist's
baptism, Luke 7:30.

Jesus and the Pharisees

- They sent the temple guard to arrest
Jesus, John 7:32, 45.
- They often tried to kill Jesus,
Matthew 12:14; John 11:47, 53.
- They imputed Jesus' miracles to
Satan's power, Matthew 9:34; 12:24.
- They condemned Jesus,
Matthew 9:11; Luke 7:39; 15:1, 2.
- They tempted Jesus, Matthew 16:1.
- Jesus compared them to
whitewashed tombs, Matthew 23:27.

"Woe to you Pharisees"

Jesus said to the teachers of the law and
to the Pharisees, "Woe to you,…you
hypocrites! You are like whitewashed
tombs, which look beautiful on the
outside but on the inside are full of dead
men's bones and everything unclean."
Matthew 23:27

Samaritans

The Samaritans were descendants of
those Jews who stayed in Palestine after
the Assyrians defeated Israel. They were
the product of mixed marriages between
the Jews and the Assyrian settlers.

- They boasted that they were
descended from Jacob, John 4:12.
- The worshiped God on Mount
Gerizim, John 4:20, where they built

a rival temple to the one in
Jerusalem. They sacrificed animals in
their temple.
- They hated the Jews, and the Jews
hated them, John 4:9; 8:48.
- Some were expecting the Messiah,
John 4:25, 29.
- Some heard and accepted the gospel,
John 4:39-42; Acts 8:4-8.
- When Jesus sent his disciples to
preach the gospel one of the places
Jesus specifically mentioned was
Samaria, Acts 1:8.
- Many churches were established in
Samaria, Acts 9:31.

Sadducees

They probably began in the Hasmonean
period, 166–63 BC. This Jewish sect
was made up of worldly-minded priests,
so when Jerusalem and the temple fell in
AD 70 they no longer had a role.

They only accepted the books of
Moses, the first five books of the Old
Testament, as scripture.

- They rejected the oral law.
- They kept the letter of the Mosaic
law, from the first five books of the
Old Testament, which they held to
be the supreme authority.
- The did not believe in the
resurrection of the dead, Matthew
22:23; Luke 20:27, or future
retribution, and denied the existence
of angels and demons, Acts 23:8.
- They were wealthy, powerful, and
lived in and around Jerusalem.

- The high priest was usually a Sadducee.
- The Sadducees hated the Pharisees, and had a public disagreement with them about the resurrection of the dead, Acts 23:6-9.
- They joined the Pharisees in their opposition to Jesus.
- John the Baptist refused to baptize them, Matthew 3:7.
- They tempted Jesus, Matthew 16:1.
- Jesus silenced the Sadducees, Matthew 22:34.

Jesus' warning about the Sadducees
"Be careful,...Be on your guard against the yeast of the Pharisees and Sadducees." *Matthew 16:6*

Essenes
They were probably formed from among the Hasidim at the same time as the Pharisees. They later split off from the Pharisees.

They became a strict and zealous Jewish sect and carefully kept the purity laws of the Torah.

They looked after each other and even shared their property with their own communities, which lived in isolated places.

There lived lives similar to monks of the Middle Ages, and while they did not ban marriage completely, they were not in favor of it for themselves. They practiced temperance and contemplation.

Covenants

EIGHT COVENANTS			
Bible reference	*Covenant*	*Participants*	*Description*
Genesis 9:8-17	Noah's covenant	God and Noah, and to Noah's descendants	God's promise never to destroy the earth again. The rainbow was the God-given sign of this covenant.
Genesis 15:9-21	Abraham's first covenant	God and Abraham, and his descendants	God's promise to give land to Abraham. "To your descendants I give this land" Genesis 15:18.
Genesis 17	Abraham's second covenant	God and Abraham, as the head of his family	The covenant of circumcision. "Every male among you shall be circumcised" Genesis 17:10.
Exodus 19–24	Covenant at Sinai	God and the people of Israel	Israel promises to be totally consecrated to God.
Numbers 25:10-31	Phinehas' covenant	God and the priest Phinehas	God promises to keep Phinehas' family as priests, so that Israel will always have a faithful priesthood.
2 Samuel 7:5-16	David's covenant	God and King David	God's promise to keep David's family on the throne of Israel.
Jeremiah 31:31-34	The new covenant	Promised to Israel when Jerusalem was about to fall	God's promise to Israel to forgive her sins and to start a new relationship with her, with the law written on her heart.
Mark 14:24	Jesus' covenant	Jesus and all who have faith in him	Jesus inaugurated this new covenant with his blood.

Stipulations of the covenant at Sinai

Laws about how people should live were given and are clearly meant for the social wellbeing of God's people. See Exodus 20:13–23:11.

"Have nothing to do with a false charge and do not put an innocent or honest person to death..." Exodus 23:7

Dreams and visions

It is sometimes difficult to distinguish between visions and dreams. However, the vision that Zachariah had in the temple, Luke 1:23, was a vivid apparition, and not a dream.

Dreams in the Old Testament

Many of the dreams recorded in the Old Testament were God's way of revealing himself, and communicating his will to people, as is seen in the dreams of:

• Jacob (Genesis 28:12; 31:10)
• Laban (Genesis 31:24)
• Joseph (Genesis 37:9-11)
• Gideon (Judges 7)
• Solomon (1 Kings 3:5)

Dreams were sent by God to a number of people who were not his followers, such as:

• Abimelech (Genesis 20:3-7)
• Pharaoh's chief butler and baker (Genesis 40:5)
• Pharaoh (Genesis 41:1-8)
• the Midianites (Judges 7:13)
• Nebuchadnezzar (Daniel 2:1; 4:10, 18)

Visions and dreams of God

Jacob dreamed about a stairway stretching from earth to heaven with angels going up and down on it. Above the stairway was the Lord, Genesis 28:12, 13.

Aaron, Nadab and Abihu, along with 70 elders of Israel "saw the God of Israel. Under his feet was something like a pavement made of sapphire, clear as the sky itself" Exodus 24:10, 11.

According to Exodus 33:23 Moses saw God's back.

Michaiah said, "I saw the Lord sitting on his throne with all the host of heaven standing on his right and on his left" 1 Chronicles 18:18.

In Isaiah's famous vision of God he saw the Lord sitting on a throne, high and exalted, Isaiah 6:1.

Ezekiel described his vision of God in the following way: "high above on the throne was a figure like that of a man" Ezekiel 1:26.

In Daniel's vision of God he identified him as "the Ancient of Days" Daniel 7:9.

As Stephen was being martyred he looked up to heaven and saw God's glory and Jesus standing at the right hand of God, Acts 7:55.

John states that in his vision of God he saw a throne in heaven with someone sitting on it, Revelation 4:2.

Dreams in the New Testament

In the New Testament most of the recorded dreams have more to do with divine guidance than with revelation about God himself. Fewer dreams are recorded in the Gospels than in the Old Testament, and no dreams are found in the New Testament letters.

• Joseph, Matthew 1:20; 2:12, 13, 19
• The wise men from the east, Matthew 2:12
• Pilate's wife, Matthew 27:19

Visions in the New Testament

- A vision of angels at Jesus' tomb, Luke 24:23
- The apostle Paul's vision of a man of Macedonia, Acts 16:9
- "One night the Lord spoke to Paul in a vision: 'Do not be afraid.'" Acts 18:9
- The apostle Paul on the Damascus Road, Acts 26:19
- The apostle Paul's vision of a speaking angel, who said, "Do not be afraid, Paul." Acts 27:23
- The apostle Paul seeing "visions and revelations from the Lord," 2 Corinthians 12:1.

A note of caution

There are a number of warnings in the Bible about not being taken in by dreams and visions being falsely interpreted.

"If there arise among you a prophet, or a dreamer of dreams, and giveth thee a sign or a wonder,

And the sign or the wonder come to pass, whereof he spake unto thee, saying, Let us go after other gods, which thou hast not known, and let us serve them;

Thou shalt not hearken unto the words of that prophet, or that dreamer of dreams: for the LORD your God proveth you, to know whether ye love the LORD your God with all your heart and with all your soul."
Deuteronomy 13:1-3 KJV

"I have heard what the prophets said, that prophesy lies in my name, saying, I have dreamed, I have dreamed.

How long shall this be in the heart of the prophets that prophesy lies? yea, they are prophets of the deceit of their own heart;

Which think to cause my people to forget my name by their dreams which they tell every man to his neighbor, as their fathers have forgotten my name for Baal."
Jeremiah 23:25-27 KJV

6 | *STRANGE BIBLE CUSTOMS,* CITED AND EXPLAINED

Introduction

Like all ancient books, the Bible describes scores of customs which are unfamiliar to us. Our understanding of a saying or biblical event can be enhanced when we know the significance of an apparently tiny piece of background information.

For example, both Mark and Luke say that Jesus told his disciples to go into Jerusalem and meet up with a man carrying a water jar (see Mark 14:13 and Luke 22:10). But the point is that in those days men did not go about carrying jars of water. This was considered to be women's work. It was like saying, "Look for a man carrying a frilly umbrella." So from this little instruction we can deduce that Jesus knew there was a mole among the disciples and made careful, and secret, arrangements about the location of his final meal.

So the more understanding we have about customs and the background life of the Bible the more understanding we have about the message of the Bible.

Bible customs: linked to Jesus

A man carrying a water jar

"Go into the city, and a man carrying a jar of water will meet you. Follow him" Mark 14:13.

Jesus gave this instruction to two of his disciples in connection with making preparations for them to eat the Passover meal together.

The habit of carrying water is an ancient one in the East. But it was work done by women. It was the woman's job to go to the well or spring with her water pot and then carry the filled pot on her head to her home.

As a punishment for deceiving Joshua the Gibeonites were made to chop wood and carry water. They were humiliated into doing women's work in public.

So when Jesus told his two disciples to follow "a man carrying a jar of water," it was not a case of which man carrying a jar of water would they follow. Rather it was a matter of following the only man they would find doing such a strange thing. While men did carry waterskins, they did not carry water jars.

Jesus' yoke

"Take my yoke upon you," Jesus told his disciples.

The yoke that Jesus refers to is probably not the yoke that harnessed two animals together for ploughing fields. Rather, it is likely to have been the kind of yoke that milkmaids used years ago when they needed to carry two pails, one balanced on each end of the yoke, which rested on her shoulders.

Jesus probably had a porter in mind when he told his disciples to take his yoke on them. The loads a porter had to carry were impossibly heavy for any person to cart around unless they were attached to a yoke. This made the job possible as it lightened the burden of the load. So Jesus did not say that he would remove burdens from his followers, but that he would give them the means to carry them – his yoke.

St Peter's fish

"Take the first fish you catch; open its mouth and you will find a four-drachma coin" Matthew 17:27. This was Jesus' instruction to Peter when Peter had been asked if Jesus paid the temple tax.

The fish that Peter caught was most probably the *tilapia* which today is commonly known as "St Peter's fish." These fish have the unusual habit of carrying their eggs in their mouths. When they are hatched they then carry their own tiny fish in their mouths. If the mother fish wants to keep her offspring out of her mouth she picks up

a bright object. The fish that Peter caught had picked up a shining shekel piece.

The two-drachma tax, Matthew 17:24, was worth half a shekel, so a shekel coin paid for Peter's and Jesus' temple tax.

The one lost coin

"Or suppose a woman has ten silver coins and loses one. Does she not light a lamp, sweep the house and search carefully until she finds it?" Luke 15:8.

It was a standard practice in the East that the bride would be given a dowry which consisted ten silver coins which were strung together and worn as part of her headdress. A wife would prize this headdress as a married woman does her wedding ring today. Should she lose even one of the coins it could be thought that she had no respect for her husband. These coins were thought of as being almost sacred and would never be spent, unless the woman became widowed and had no other money.

A cup of water

"Anyone who gives you a cup of water in my name because you belong to Christ will certainly not lose his reward" Mark 9:41.

Jesus is assuring his disciples here that even a small act of kindness done to his followers because they are his followers will not go unremembered.

When a guest entered a person's house he was given a cup of cold water to drink to refresh him. This simple act was sometimes taken as a sign of friendship. This accounts for Eliezer, Abraham's servant, who expected a drink of water as part of his welcome, Genesis 24:17, 18.

Bible customs: linked to animals, trees and plants

trod on the grain with their sharp hooves. The root meaning of the Hebrew word for "thresh" is "to trample." According to the law, when an ox was treading out grain it was not to be muzzled so that it could eat some grain when it became hungry. The principle that a laborer is worthy of his hire applied even to animals in the Old Testament.

This way of threshing was adapted at a later stage when the threshing sledge was invented. The oxen were hitched to the threshing sledge and they pulled it along behind them over the grain. Long planks of wood were fixed to each other side by side. Underneath the sledge flint stones were fastened with pitch. The grain fell through the straw on the hard ground while the straw lay on the surface.

Paul applied this principle to ministers of Christ and wrote that those who worked by preaching the gospel should live by the gospel, 1 Corinthians 9:9-10; 1 Timothy 5:17, 18.

Muzzling an ox

"Do not muzzle an ox while it is treading out the grain" Deuteronomy 25:4.

When God made his covenant with Noah and all humankind that would follow, the animals were not left out. In the Ten Commandments animals are to be looked after. Oxen were used to thresh the grain. A pair of oxen were yoked together and attached to the yoke, which was a vertical pole fixed to the center of the threshing floor. As the oxen moved round in an endless circle they

Purged by a hyssop

"Cleanse me with hyssop" Psalm 51:7.

The small plant, hyssop, was grown for its medicinal oil and as a spice. It was noted for cleansing the digestive tract of anyone who ate it, and so it was linked to internal cleansing. Although it was also used for external purification, Leviticus 14:1-7; Numbers 19:1-19, David, in this penitential psalm, had in mind being cleansed from his sin.

A palm tree

"The righteous will flourish like a palm tree" Psalm 92:11.

These palm trees grew to a height of 80 or 90 feet and had straight trunks from the ground to its bunched, feathery leaves. It produced dates which were particularly appreciated for their sweetness. It withstood the worst sand storms of the desert as it had such strong roots which were adapted to seek out moisture from the ground in a most efficient way. It needed little if any cultivation during the 30 years it took to become mature. Often they lived for over 200 years. Their leaves were used for roofing, and it was their branches that were waved in welcome when Jesus entered Jerusalem, John 12:12, 13. Its crown was woven into rope. The date palm tree made a good illustration of a fruitful believer as it was excellent at producing fruit.

A cedar of Lebanon

"...they will grow like a cedar of Lebanon; planted in the house of the Lord, they will flourish in the courts of our God" Psalm 92:11.

To be compared with a cedar of Lebanon would be praise indeed. For certain building projects, like Solomon's temple, this wood was prized above all other woods. These trees grew to a height of 70 or 80 feet and once covered Lebanon's western slopes. Their girths extended to 30 or 40 feet. This warm, red wood, is free of knots, and has a fragrance which is pleasant to humans, but repels insects. It was in every way an ideal wood for large buildings and for building ships. To be a cedar of Lebanon a believer would have to be sturdy.

Bible customs: linked to clothes

Joseph's coat of "many colors"

"Israel...made a richly ornamented robe for him [Joseph]" Genesis 37:3.

The *King James Version* tells us that Jacob (Israel) made Joseph "a coat of many colors." Rather than being made of many colors, one of the distinguishing features of this coat may have been its long sleeves. A coat with long sleeves was not one to wear if you wanted to do any manual work as the sleeves got in the way. This kind of coat could only be worn by two people in a tribe – either the head of the tribe, or the appointed heir of the tribe. Usually the heir would be the eldest son, but here Jacob is choosing his youngest but one son to be his heir. It is no wonder that Joseph's brothers were so jealous of him and this was only increased by this mark of Jacob's favoritism. According to 2 Samuel 13:18 this kind of richly ornamented robe was "the kind of garment the virgin daughters of the king wore."

Put on sackcloth

"When Mordecai learned of all that had been done, he tore his clothes, put on sackcloth and ashes, and went out into the city, wailing loudly and bitterly" Esther 4:1.

Sackcloth was made from coarse, heavy, dark cloth from goats' hair. Hence when Mordecai learned that the royal decree said that all the Jews were to be destroyed, killed and annihilated, he put on sackcloth to show the depth of his mourning.

At Abner's funeral David gave orders that everyone should tear their clothes and wear sackcloth and mourn, 2 Samuel 3:31. When the time to take off sackcloth came it was a time for joy and rejoicing, Psalm 30:11, 12.

With your loins girded

"This is how you are to eat it: with your cloak tucked into your belt, your sandals on your feet and your staff in your hand" Exodus 12:11.

The *King James Version* of this verse has "with your loins girded." In Bible times the loincloth was the undergarment worn by men. When Peter was "naked" or "stripped for action" in John 21:7 as

This alludes to a state of readiness, not sitting around idly with loose and impractical clothes.

Cloak and tunic

In New Testament days men wore tunics which looked rather like sacks with three slits for the head and two arms. Over the tunic rich people wore cloaks which were like loose-fitting dressing-gowns, with long flowing sleeves.

In Matthew 5:40 Jesus said that if someone wants to sue and take your tunic give him your cloak as well, since in law you could not take away a person's cloak. But in Luke 6:29 Jesus was not muddled up when he said if someone takes your cloak, do not stop him from taking your tunic. For in the latter case a robber is in mind who would grab the first thing that came to hand, a cloak.

he was fishing he would have been wearing a loincloth. Jesus' tunic had been removed by the soldiers when he was crucified, John 19:23, so he would have only been left wearing a loincloth.

The loincloth consisted of a long piece of cloth, not unlike a shawl, which was folded around the waist. It could also be used for keeping long loose robes out of the way, as they could be tucked into the loincloth, which the *NIV* translates in Exodus 12:11 as "with your cloak tucked into your belt."

Paul says that the correctly dressed believer should "stand...having your loins girt about with truth" *KJV*, "stand firm them, with the belt of truth buckled round your waist" Ephesians 6:14 *NIV*.

Bible customs: linked to food and water

Like a bottle in the smoke

"Though I am like a wineskin in the smoke, I do not forget your decrees" Psalm 119:83.

The equivalent to a bottle in Palestine was not made of glass but was a goatskin. After the animal had been killed the feet and head were cut off and the carcass was drawn out of the skin by turning the skin inside out. The skin was then tanned and all the openings, except for one of the feet were sewn together. It was then ready to be filled with wine or water.

These wineskins were hung up and the smoke from the cooking fires soon dried and blackened them. The smoke and the heat of the fire eventually made these wineskins smudged and shriveled. That is just how the psalmist said he felt.

Covenant of salt

"It is an everlasting covenant of salt before the Lord for both you and your offspring" Numbers 18:19.

Eating salt with someone was an act of friendship in ancient days. Each person who wanted to join in this covenant would wet his finger with his tongue, dip his finger into the salt, and eat the salt. This was a binding covenant which should never be forgotten or renounced. Hence 2 Chronicles 13:5 states, "Don't you know that the Lord, the God of Israel, has given the kingship of Israel to David and his descendants forever by a covenant of salt?"

Salt also had to accompany grain offerings and was called the "salt of the covenant," Leviticus 2:13. Salt had to be sprinkled on burnt offerings, Ezekiel 43:24, and was one of the ingredients of the incense used in the sanctuary, Exodus 30:35.

The "covenant of salt" may also refer to the salt that was used in the sacrificial meal that often accompanied the making of a covenant, Genesis 31:54.

Picking ears of corn

"If you enter your neighbor's cornfield, you may pick the ears with your hand, but you must not put a sickle to his standing corn" Deuteronomy 23:25.

If a person was on a journey and was near a field at lunchtime the law stated that he was allowed to eat the fruit of the field until he was no longer hungry. However, he was not allowed to take

extra grapes or corn in any container or
to fill his pockets with food. This law
gave Jesus' disciples the right to pluck
ears of corn and eat them,
Matthew 12:1.

Salt trampled by men

"You are the salt of the earth. But if the
salt loses its saltiness, how can it be
made salty again? It is no longer good
for anything, except to be thrown out
and trampled under by men"
Matthew 5:13.

Salt, used for flavoring and as a
preservative, was collected from the area
around the Dead Sea. Salt that had lost
its saltiness was not just thrown away
but was stored in the temple in
Jerusalem. Then, when the winter rains
made the marble slippery, this salt was
spread out on the marble to prevent
people from falling over. In this way salt
that had lost its saltiness was trampled
under foot by people.

Sifted like wheat

"Simon, Simon, Satan has asked to sift
you as wheat" Luke 22:31.

Women formed a circle and used clubs
to beat wheat with as it lay on the
threshing floor so that the kernel was
separated from the stalks. Then, every so
often, a couple of men would come, and
using wooden pitchforks, they scooped
all the stalks and kernels into the air.
The wind blew away the lighter ears of
corn and stalks, but the heavier kernels
fell straight to the ground.

This verse shows that Satan wanted to
spiritually ruin the disciples by testing
them. In the Greek the word for "you" is
in the plural, so it is assumed that this
Satanic attack was against all the
disciples and not just Peter.

Bible customs: found in the Old Testament

The weaning of Samuel

"After he [Samuel] was weaned, she [Hannah] took the boy with her, young as he was,…and brought him to the house of the Lord at Shiloh"
1 Samuel 1:24.

Hannah took Samuel to the house of the Lord at Shiloh after she had weaned him, as a "boy," that is a young child, but not as a baby. In the Near East children, especially boys, are not weaned until they are three or four years old, or, until they are even older. In Bible times there was no way to store milk. It is clear from a reference in the Apocrypha that this was a normal practice: "My son, have pity on me. I carried you for nine months in my womb, and nursed you for three years..." 2 Maccabees 7:27 *NRSV*.

Greet no one

"Elisha said to Gehazi, 'Tuck your cloak into your belt, take my staff in your hand and run. If you meet anyone, do not greet him, and if anyone greets you, do not answer. Lay my staff on the boy's face'" 2 Kings 4:29.

In the Near East greeting someone is seen as an act of courtesy. But it is more than a wave of the hand to someone across the street. It is more than a handshake. It involves falling on a person's neck and kissing both checks. Then there would be an exchange of greetings. After that each would enquire about the other's family, but not in a general way, but each member of the family was to be asked after. This would include the wife, each child, and then the extended family: the sons-in-law, the daughters-in-law, the grandparents, and the uncles and aunts. It was quite a time-consuming event. As Gehazi was on an urgent errand of mercy Elisha told him that he should greet no one.

In the same way, when Jesus sent out the 70 he told them: "Do not greet anyone on the road" Luke 10:4.

Hagar and Ishmael

"Now Sarai, Abram's wife, had borne him no children. But she had an Egyptian maidservant named Hagar; so she said to Abram, 'The Lord has kept me from having children. Go, sleep with my maidservant; perhaps I can build a family through her'" Genesis 16:1, 2.

When Sarai gave Abram her servant Hagar to bear a child Sarai was only following the custom of the day. This custom is recorded in Old Assyrian marriage contracts, the *Nuzi* tablets, which are from the mid-second millennium BC, and the *Code of Hammurabi*. These state that if a wife could have no children she should give her slave girl as a wife for her husband. But if the wife later bore a child, the wife was not allowed to drive away the slave-wife. This might explain Abraham's reluctance over having to send Hagar and Ishmael way when God commanded him to do this.

Landmarks

"'Cursed is the man who moves his neighbor's boundary stone'" Deuteronomy 27:17.

In the Old Testament people erected a pile of stones to indicate the boundary of their land. The stones were placed on top of each other until they were about two feet high. If these landmarks were moved so that one could increase the area of one's own fields or estates it was deemed to be a serious crime.

Fine perfume

"A good name is better than fine perfume" Ecclesiastes 7:1.

Eastern perfumes and ointments were very expensive and were kept in precious vases and jars made of alabaster stone or metal. People loved to own such perfume and use it on themselves. Perfumed oil was put on the body to mask bad odors or to soften the skin, Ruth 3:3; Psalm 45:8; Ezekiel 16:9. Perfumed oil was poured over the feet or heads of people attending a banquet, 2 Chronicles 16:14. However, Solomon is saying in Ecclesiastes that a person who had deserved to have a good reputation became the envy of his neighbors.

Bible customs: linked to family life

Ruth clung to Naomi

"Then Orpah kissed her mother-in-law good-bye, but Ruth clung to her" Ruth 1:14.

In Bible times some people showed remarkable loyalty to their family and to the religion of their family. It was definitely politically incorrect to break with one's family. So when Ruth decided to comfort Naomi and to return with her to Bethlehem, Ruth was making a decisive break with her own family and religion, for she was a Moabite, Ruth 1:4.

The targum, an Aramaic commentary on the Old Testament, on Ruth 1:12-17 explains Ruth's faithfulness to Naomi.

- "And Ruth said, 'Entreat me not to leave you, for I want to become a proselyte.'"
- "And Naomi said, 'We are commanded to keep the Sabbath and other holy days, and on it not to travel more than 2000 cubits.'"
- "And Ruth said, 'Wherever you go, I will go.'"
- "And Naomi said, 'We are commanded not to stay with Gentiles.'"
- "Ruth answered, 'Wherever you live, I will live.'"
- "And Naomi said, 'We are commanded to observe the 113 precepts.'"
- "Ruth answered, 'What your people observe, I will observe, as if the precepts had been the precepts of my own people.'"
- "And Naomi said, 'We are commanded not to worship any foreign gods.'"
- "Ruth answered, 'Your God will be my God.'"
- "Naomi said, 'It is our custom, if at all possible, to be buried in our own country.'"
- "Ruth answered, 'Where you die, I will die.'"
- "Naomi said, 'We have a family burial plot.'"
- "Ruth answered, 'And there I will be buried also.'"

Not to be rubbed with salt or wrapped in cloths were signs of a baby being neglected. Not to follow these customs was unheard of in Bible times. As late as the beginning of the twentieth century the practice of rubbing new born babies with salt continued. After new born babies had been rubbed in salt they were bound up tightly in strips of cloth as this was meant to keep the baby strong. If the limbs were tightly bound Jewish mothers believed that their babies would grow straight. These strips of cloth were four or five inches wide and 15 to 18 feet long. Hence Mary wrapped Jesus in cloths before placing him in a manger, Luke 2:7.

Beds

"Let the saints…sing for joy on their beds" Psalm 149:5.

In the East in Bible times the bed was not a piece of furniture but a mat. Whole families slept on a single mat together. In the morning the mat was rolled up so that it did not take up so much space. People could, and did, quite easily take their "beds" around with them. Hence Jesus says to a man he had just healed: "Get up, take your mat and go home" Matthew 9:6.

New born babies

"On the day you were born your cord was not cut, nor were you washed with water to make you clean, nor were you rubbed with salt or wrapped in cloths" Ezekiel, 16:4.

Many rooms

"In my Father's house are many rooms" John 14:2.

In the Old Testament a newly married couple was encouraged to spend a year-long honeymoon at the homes of their families: "For one year he [a recently married man] is to be free to stay at home and bring happiness to the wife he has married" Deuteronomy 24:5. Then the son would often work in the fields which belonged to his father. There would be several houses on the family estate. So the husband could say to his wife, "In my father's house (on my father's estate) there are many apartments. I am going to prepare a place for you. I will come back to you and bring you along so that where I live you may live."

Bible customs: linked to death

Mummification

"Then Joseph directed the physicians in his service to embalm his father Israel. So the physicians embalmed him, taking a full forty days, for that was the time required for embalming" Genesis 50:2, 3.

Egypt's method of embalming was mummification, a 40-day, and sometimes a 70-day process. The abdomen was cut open, the internal organs removed, and then the abdomen was rinsed with palm wine, before it was filled with perfumes, spices and oils. Then the physicians sewed up the body, washed it, wrapped it up in a flaxen cloth and placed it in a coffin.

From this it is possible to see how Joseph could go on a long journey back to Canaan with his father's body, Genesis 50:4-13.

Let me bury my father

"He [Jesus] said to another man, 'Follow me.' But the man replied, 'Lord, first let me go and bury my father.' Jesus said to him, 'Let the dead bury their own dead, but you go and proclaim the kingdom of God'" Luke 9:59, 60.

At first sight it may appear that Jesus is being somewhat harsh in the way he spoke with this man. If someone was in the middle of a funeral service that was no time to make demands on him. But the point here is that the man's father was not yet dead. If he had been the man would have been arranging his funeral and not speaking with Jesus.

But the man said he wanted to wait until his father died, and that might be in several years' time. It is possible that the man was his father's eldest son, in which case he would be the heir of all his father's possessions. In any case Jesus told him, in effect, that the spiritually dead should be left to bury the physically dead, while the spiritually alive should be engaged in preaching about the kingdom of God.

The burial of Jesus

"[John] outran Peter and reached the tomb first. He bent over and looked in at the strips of linen lying there but did not go in. Then Simon Peter, who was behind him arrived and went into the tomb. He saw the strips of linen lying there, as well as the burial cloth that had been around Jesus' head. The cloth was folded up by itself, separate from the linen. Finally, the other disciple, who had reached the tomb first, also went inside. He saw and believed" John 20:4-8.

Jesus' body had been wrapped up in strips of linen together with 75 pounds of myrrh and aloes and with spices, John 19:39, 40. Looking in from the outside it must have looked like a cocoon and would have retained the shape of a body, even though Jesus' body was no longer there. This is the reason for Peter and John seeing the tomb and only upon entering it did they believe in the resurrection of Jesus. Clearly the body had not been stolen because the bandages were not unwrapped.

John would have looked into the tomb from the outside, seen the cocoon and deduced that Jesus' body was still there. So John did not enter the tomb then, even though he outran Peter to the tomb. When Peter arrived at the tomb he went straight in. Then John went in. Then they saw that there was a gap where Jesus' face should have been.

Then they realized what had happened. Just as Jesus' would later pass through the locked door and come into the room where Thomas and the other ten disciples were, so Peter and John now believed that Jesus' body had passed through the spice-impregnated bandages. His body had not been stolen. Jesus had risen.

Bible customs: linked to puzzling words and phrases

Irrigated by foot

"The land you are entering to take over is not like the land of Egypt, from which you have come, where you planted your seed and irrigated it by foot as in a vegetable garden" Deuteronomy 11:10.

In the East water was often very scarce and only available at one point. Shallow gullies or trenches were made throughout the area that was under cultivation and then filled with water from the main source. When a particular area needed water a man would walk along the trench and flatten the existing rills with his foot. Then the water flowed to the area of dry land. Sometimes even the original channels for the water were dug by foot. The foot was also used to work devices which lifted the water from the river Nile to the vegetation and gardens of Egypt.

Coals of fire

"If your enemy is hungry, feed him; if he is thirsty, give him something to drink. In doing this, you will heap burning coals on his head" Romans 12:20.

In Bible lands nearly everything was carried on the head: jars, fruit, vegetables. Outside the house cooking was done on small burners. If your own fire went out it was quite normal to take your brazier to a neighbor who would fill it with burning coals, and then you would carry the brazier with the burning coals in it on your head back to your own home. This action depicts neighborliness and warm friendship.

To heap burning coals on an enemy's head would be showing kindness, even though he was an enemy. This might have the effect of searing his conscience if he was guilty and make him repent in the presence of such love and forgiveness. Doing good to one's enemy, rather than taking revenge on him might bring about his repentance. Kindness can win an enemy over.

Heaping burning coals on a head also speaks of judgment. The psalmist says, "Let burning coals fall upon them" Psalm 140:10, longing for God's judgment to fall on his enemies, perhaps recalling God's judgment on Sodom and Gomorrah.

Oil and shining faces

"...oil to make his face shine" Psalm 104:15.

The oil mentioned here is olive oil. In the Old Testament oil was used for a variety of purposes, such as anointing for consecration and as a sign of joy. Sacred oil for the purpose of anointing was made by adding liquid myrrh, fragrant cinnamon, fragrant cane, and cassia to olive oil, Exodus 30:22, 23. When guests arrived at a social function they would have their foreheads anointed with oil.

Olive oil was also used in baking bread, 1 Kings 17:12, and was reputed to make a person's face shine with health. Oil, in this case oil of myrrh, was used as a cosmetic, for six months, by all the girls who were presented to King Xerxes as potential brides, Esther 2:12.

Psalm 104 is full of God's wonderful attributes: his goodness, his kindness, and his love. They are like an anointing of joy to the psalmist, like oil that makes his face shine.

Writing on the ground

"They were using this question as a trap in order to have a basis for accusing him. But Jesus bent down and started to write on the ground with his finger" John 8:6.

To write something on the ground with one's finger was a common practice. Sometimes little drawings were sketched out in the dusty ground. Arabs who were bargaining for animals or food would do their calculations with their fingers in the sand. During a hearing at a city gate an elder would scribble a word or two in the sand with his finger which might make the others sit up and take notice.

Nobody knows what Jesus wrote on the ground when he was being asked if the woman in front of him should be stoned to death for adultery. After he had written something, Jesus said, "If any one of you is without sin, let him be the first to throw a stone at her." Then John records that Jesus stooped down again and started to write on the ground again. Whatever he wrote, this writing and Jesus' words had the effect of making all the woman's accusers go away. The eldest left first, until Jesus was alone with the woman.

Bible customs: magical arts

Detestable practices

"Let no one be found among you who sacrifices his son or daughter in the fire, who practices divination or sorcery, interprets omens, engages in witchcraft, or casts spells, or who is a medium or spiritist or who consults the dead" Deuteronomy 18:10-12.

This is the most complete list of spiritist or magical arts found in the Old Testament. These practices were all found in Canaan. Each one is condemned and God's people were told not to engage in them, Deuteronomy 18:14.

Human sacrifice

"They even burn their sons and daughters in the fire as sacrifices to their gods" Deuteronomy 12:31.

"Do not give any of your children to be sacrificed to Molech, for you must not profane the name of your God. I am the Lord" Leviticus 18:21.

In Phoenicia and the surrounding countries the practice of child sacrifice to Molech, the god of the Ammonites, was common. It is clear that Manasseh sacrificed his sons to Molech, 2 Chronicles 33:6. Jeremiah spoke out against this most evil practice, Jeremiah 32:35.

Divination

Divination involves trying to find out about the future by consulting supernatural sources or by observing omens. It may be distinguished from magic which attempts to control events. Divining is concerned with learning about the future so one can take appropriate action.

The Mesopatamians studied the livers of sacrificial animals. They looked for omens in the shape and texture of each section. Their *baru*-priests even used written interpretations to consult as they searched for omens. The Greeks and Romans studied the flight of birds or the entrails of birds as they sought for omens.

King Saul went to the witch of Endor who was also a medium. Saul consulted her in his quest to find help from the dead Samuel, 1 Samuel 28.

ANCIENT METHODS OF DIVINATION		
Name	*Meaning*	*Bible reference*
Astrology	The study of the supposed influence of stars	Isaiah 47:13; Jeremiah 10:2
Hepatoscopy	Reading the livers of sheep or goats	
Hydromancy	Using water to divine	Genesis 44:5, 15
Lots	Used by groups in decision making	Leviticus 16:18; Numbers 26:55, 56; Esther 9:24-26; Jonah 1:7; Matthew 27:35; Acts 1:26
Necromancy	Consulting the dead	Leviticus 19:31; 20:6; Deuteronomy 18:11; 1 Samuel 28:8; 2 Kings 21:6; 2 Chronicles 10:13; Isaiah 8:19, 20
Oneiromancy	Seeking guidance from dreams	Genesis 40:1-40; Jeremiah 23:25-27; Daniel 4:1-18
Rhabdomancy	Studying thrown sticks or arrows	2 Kings 13:14-19; Ezekiel 21:21; Hosea 4:12

Bible customs: linked to God's judgment and forgiveness

Urim and Thummim

"Also put the Urim and the Thummim in the breastplate, so they may be over Aaron's heart whenever he enters the presence of the Lord. Thus Aaron will always bear the means of making decisions for the Israelites over his heart before the Lord" Exodus 28:30.

It is not completely clear how the Urim and Thummin was used but it is clear that God commanded them to be used and that he communicated through them on special occasions.

Aaron, and successive high priests, wore a canvas bag on his chest, on the outside of which was the golden breastplate with the 12 precious stones, each one representing one of the 12 tribes of Israel. Inside the canvas bag were two lots which may have been disc-shaped, colored black on one side and white on the other. It is possible that the way Urim and Thummin worked was that when the two lots were cast from the bag two whites meant "yes," two blacks meant "no," and a black and a white meant "wait."

Winepress

"In his winepress the Lord has trampled the Virgin Daughter of Judah" Lamentations 1:15.

The winepress is a common metaphor for divine judgment in the Old Testament, Isaiah 63:2-3; Joel 3:13, and in the New Testament, Revelation 14:19-20; 19:15.

Many homes had their own winepress or were familiar with using one. It was a cistern cut out of rock with a small hole at one end or in the bottom. It could be as small as five feet long and ten inches deep. Ripe grapes were put in it and crushed by the feet of those treading them. The juice ran into the hole where it was collected by a vat or a wineskin. In larger winepresses many people would be involved in treading the grapes and would hang on to overhanging branches to help them keep their balance.

Millstones

"But if anyone causes one of these little ones who believe in me to sin, it would be better for him to have a large millstone hung around his neck and to be drowned in the depths of the sea" Matthew 18:6.

The particular millstone in Matthew 18:6 is, literally, "the millstone of a donkey." This is to differentiate it from the hand millstones which were less that two feet wide and were used for grinding corn. This millstone was the millstone that was turned by a donkey and was much larger and heavier. These larger rotary millstones were turned by animals or prisoners. The blinded Samson was "set to grinding in the prison" Judges 16:21.

One method of capital punishment in the Graeco-Roman world was to bind a millstone to a condemned man's neck and then throw him into the sea. Jesus was teaching how important it was that trusting and unpretentious believers, the "little ones," should not be led astray or made to sin by anyone.

The scapegoat

"But the goat, on which the lot fell to be the scapegoat, shall be presented alive before the Lord, to make an atonement with him, and to let him go for a scapegoat into the wilderness" Leviticus 16:10 KJV.

We call someone who is made to take the blame for the actions of other people a scapegoat. The English word is derived from the words "escape" and "goat." A scapegoat was originally the goat that symbolically carried all the sins of Israel and was sent off into the desert. John 1:29 speaks of Jesus as the lamb of God taking away the sins of the world, and Isaiah speaks of a lamb being led to the slaughter, Isaiah 53:7. From Leviticus 16:10 it is also right to picture Jesus acting as a scapegoat on behalf of us.

The scapegoat is only mentioned in Leviticus chapter 16. It was one of two goats, and the other goat was killed as a sacrifice. On the Day of Atonement,

when the scapegoat was released, God's people were encouraged to see how their sins had been, symbolically, taken way by the scapegoat.

There is a similar ceremony to the one recorded in Leviticus chapter 14. It concerned a person who had recovered from leprosy. This time there were two birds, one of which was killed as a sacrifice. Then, at the end of the ceremony, the other bird was released into the fields and symbolically took with him the leper's disease.

Book of life

"May they be blotted out of the book of life and not be listed with the righteous" Psalm 69:28.

In the Old Testament the book of life is a symbolic book which God has in which are written a list of all the righteous people whom God blesses, Psalm 1:3; 7:9; 11:7; 34:12; 37:17, 29; 55:22; 75:10; 92:12-14; 140:13.

In the New Testament the book of life is a similar book. This time it is a list of all those who are destined for eternal life, Philippians 4:3; Revelation 3:5; 13:8; 17:8; 20:12, 15; 21:27.

Bible customs: linked to God's care

Carrying a lamb

"He tends his flock like a shepherd:
He gathers the lambs in his arms
and carries them close to his heart;
he gently leads those that have young"
Isaiah 40:11.

A shepherd often takes a tired lamb, especially very young ones, into his arms. Then in the folds of his large outer robe he carries it, so that it is "close to his heart." In this way the shepherd's hands are still free to do other work. Meanwhile the lamb rests secure and snug as a result of the personal care of the shepherd. Jesus used similar imagery in John 10 when he described himself as the "good Shepherd."

Signet ring

"I will make you my signet ring, for I have chosen you" Haggai 2:23.

The signet ring was used as a stamp or seal on documents. Documents were not considered to be legal unless they had a seal on them. The signet ring also served as a signature, see Esther 8:8. In Haggai the Lord tells Zerubbabel that he will be like a signet ring. So as he stood before the people he was assured that he had the stamp of God's authority on him.

In the New Testament a seal is mentioned in connection with the Holy Spirit who guarantees the believer's future inheritance, 2 Corinthians 1:22.

Engraved on the palms of my hand

"See, I have engraved you on the palms of my hands" Isaiah 49:16.

The names of each of the 12 tribes of Israel were engraved on the stones on the outside of the high priest's ephod as a memorial before the Lord. In the same way the Lord says in Isaiah 49:16 that he will never forget his people.

When a son left home it used to be a custom for Palestinian women to have something tatooed on the palm of her hand to remind her of her son. A mother with such a tatoo never forgot her son.

Between his shoulders

"The one the Lord loves rests between his shoulders" Deuteronomy 33:12.

When a mother carried her child the child was strapped to her back between her shoulders, so that her hands and arms were free to work in the fields. In the same way the Lord has bound his followers to himself.

Like an eagle

"...like an eagle that stirs up its nest and hovers over its young, that spreads its wings to catch them and carries them on its pinions" Deuteronomy 32:11.

One of the three things that was too wonderful for the writer of Proverbs was the way of an eagle in the sky, Proverbs 30:18, 19. The seemingly effortless flight of the eagle inspired Isaiah to use it as an image of God's people who rise up as their hope is in God and soar into the sky like an eagle, Isaiah 40:31: "...those who hope in the Lord will renew their strength. They will soar on wings like eagles."

Eagles were known for their vigor, "your youth is renewed as the eagle's" Psalm 103:5, and for their speed, "...his horses are swifter than eagles" Jeremiah 4:13.

Eagles built their nests on high

mountain crags so that their young would be safe. This meant that there was no ground nearby where their young could learn to fly. So when the time was right the adult eagle nudged the baby eagle out of the nest so that it fell downwards in the air. As the young eagle started to try to use its wings to fly the adult eagle was continually following it. When the young eagle grew tired the adult eagle simply flew below it, spread out its wings and the young eagle was given a ride back to its nest.

7 UNRAVELING BIBLE SYMBOLS

Introduction

Three Israelis, Doron Witztum, Eliyahu Rips and Yoav Rosenberg (WRR) hit the headlines when they claimed that there was serious scientific evidence for Bible Codes (also called Torah Codes). They asserted that the Hebrew text of the Bible contained intentional coincidences of words or phrases that appeared as letters with equal spacing. From this they deduced that biographical information about medieval rabbis was encoded in the Hebrew text of Genesis.

The first serious attack on WRR's claims was published by mathematicians Dror Bar-Natan and Brendan McKay who showed that they could obtain similar results from the novel *War and Peace*. In a scholarly way they were saying that the alleged scientific evidence for these codes in the Bible was bunk.

This chapter does not find any one code in the Bible but it does offer explanations about many intriguing symbols, symbolic numbers, like 666, and secret signs which are contained in the pages of the Bible.

It also explains why many of the much-loved and convoluted allegorical interpretations of the Bible, (held by some early church Fathers, medieval theologians and adopted by some Reformers) are erroneous.

Figures of speech

In common with most literature the Bible employs numerous figures of speech. These need to be identified, or else we run the danger of making serious mistakes in our interpretation of Scripture.

Hyperbole

A hyperbole presents something as being much greater or smaller than it is.

Israel are like "grasshoppers" in the presence of "giants," Numbers 13:33.

The city walls of Canaan stretch up to the sky, Deuteronomy 1:28.

Irony

Irony is a figure of speech that uses words to express something different from and often opposite to their literal meaning. There are just a few examples of irony in the Bible.

Elijah taunting the priests of Baal about the god Baal, 1 Kings 18:27.

Job remarking to his friends that wisdom will die with them, Job 12:2.

Metaphor

A metaphor is a figure of speech in which a word or phrase that usually means one thing is used to mean something else.

James writes about bridling the tongue, James 1:26.

Deuteronomy 32:42 speaks of arrows being drunk with blood.

Metonymy

A metonymy is a figure of speech in which one word is put for another.

When it is said in Luke 16:29: "They have Moses and the Prophets," the word "Prophets" does not refer to the people who were prophets but to their writings.

Parable

See *Parables and Allegories*, p 171.

Personification

A personification attributes the actions of people to things.

"Love and faithfulness meet together; righteousness and peace kiss each other" Psalm 85:10.

Synecdoche

A synecdoche puts a part for the whole of something, or the whole of something for a part.

Acts 27:37 (*KJV*) refers to 276 "souls," when it clearly means people, and in this example "souls" stand for the whole person.

Parables and allegories

Allegory

An allegory is an extended metaphor, such as Jesus' teaching about eating his flesh, John 6:35-36. John's gospel is full of such allegories.

Allegorical interpretations

In the past some Bible commentators have gone overboard when they have attempted to interpret parables in the Bible in an allegorical way. For example, Augustine's (350–430) allegorical interpretation of the parable of the Sower (Luke 10:30-37) goes as follows:

- the wounded man stands for Adam
- Jerusalem: the heavenly city from which he has fallen
- the thieves: the devil who strips Adam of his immortality and leads him to sin
- the priest and Levite: the Old Testament Law and ministry which was unable to cleanse and save anyone
- the good Samaritan who binds the wounds: Christ who forgives sin
- oil and wine: hope and stimulus to work
- the animal: the incarnation
- the inn: the church
- and the innkeeper: the apostle

Parables

The term parable (*mashal* in the Old Testament, and *parabolea* in the New Testament) is used in a variety of ways in Scripture. It can refer to:

- a proverb (1 Samuel 24:13)
- a satire or taunt (Psalm 44:11)
- a riddle (Psalm 49:4)
- a figurative saying (Mark 7:14-17)
- an extended simile (Matthew 13:33)
- a story parable (Matthew 25:1-13)
- an example parable (Matthew 18:23-25)
- an allegory (Judges 9:7-20; Mark 4:3-9, 13-20).

In each of the parables something known is compared with something unknown in order to shed light on the latter.

Symbolism in John's Gospel

John is full of profound mysteries and comparisons, and has rightly been called the "spiritual" Gospel. John achieves this in numerous ways. One straightforward way is through the frequent comparisons he makes.

- The temple and the body, John 2:25
- Water and the Spirit, John 7:37-38

John's symbolism sometimes takes the form of dualistic antitheses:

- light is compared with darkness (1:4; 3:19; 8:12; 11:9; 12:35, 46)
- truth is compared with falsehood (8:44)
- life is compared with death (5:24; 11:25)
- above is compared with below (8:23)
- freedom is compared with slavery (8:33, 36).

Symbolic language: A to C

A

Adulteress (harlot) Apostate city *Isaiah 1:21*, Apostate church *Revelation 17:5*

Abominations Sin in general *Proverbs 26:25*

Air Moral influences *Ephesians 2:2*

Almonds Spirit-produced fruit *Numbers 17:8*

Anchor Confidence and security *Hebrews 6:19*

Angels Ministers of God's providence *Hebrews 1:4-7*, Pastors *Revelation 1:20*, Apostate spirits *Matthew 25:41*

Animals

> **Beast/s** The wicked *Psalm 49:20*, The Antichrist *Revelation 13:2*
>
> **Deer** Surefootedness of Christians *Psalm 18:33*
>
> **Donkey** Humility *Matthew 21:7*
>
> **Fox** Deceit and craftiness *Luke 13:32*
>
> **Horse** A headstrong attitude *Psalm 32:9*
>
> **Lion** Christ *Revelation 5:5*, Satan *1 Peter 5:8*, The tribe of Judah *Genesis 49:9*, Courage *2 Samuel 17:10*, Boldness of Christians *Proverbs 18:1*
>
> **Pigs** The wicked *Matthew 7:6*
>
> **Sheep** Followers of Jesus *John 10:7-26*, Restored sinner *Luke 15:5, 7*, The unregenerate *Matthew 10:6*
>
> **Wolf** Fierce enemy *Luke 10:3*, False teachers *Acts 20:29*

Anoint Consecrate, appoint, confer power *Leviticus 8:10-12; Acts 10:38*

ANTHROPOMORPHISM

This literary device speaks of God, or animals, or objects in human terms.

In Exodus 33:20 God says that his face cannot be seen.

According to 1 Timothy 6:16 God lives in unapproachable light

In Exodus 31:18 we read that the Ten Commandments were written on stone tablets by the finger of God. So the question arises: Do we have to believe that a divine finger literally inscribed Hebrew letters on stone?

In other parts of the Bible there are other references to God's fingers and they are symbolical. David refers to the heavens as the work of God's fingers, Psalm 8:3. Another example is after the plague of gnats the Egyptian magicians tell Pharaoh that this happened through the finger of God, Exodus 8:19. A third example is when Jesus claimed to cast out demons by the finger of God, Luke 11:20.

From this it would be fair to conclude that the phrase "the finger of God" is a biblical figure of speech standing for God's immediate action and intervention.

Ark Center of divine strength *Psalm 132:8*, Relationship with God *Revelation 11:19*

Arm, outstretched arm. God's omnipotence *Jeremiah 27:5*

Armor Spiritual strength *Ephesians 6:11*

Ashes Humiliation *Job 42:6*

B

Balaam Impurity leading to backsliding
2 Peter 2:15
Bees Many enemies *Deuteronomy 1:44*

BIBLICAL IMAGES OF THE CHURCH

THE CHURCH AS BODY OF CHRIST

The church relates to Jesus as its head,
and members of the church are living
members of the body of Christ. God
gives spiritual gifts which are intended
to build up other Christians.

Key scriptures are: 1 Corinthians
12:12-31; Ephesians 1:22; 4:1-6;
Colossians 1:18.

THE CHURCH AS THE FAMILY OF GOD

The church is a family in which God
the Father is the leader, and Christians
are each others brothers and sisters,
who are supposed to live a life of love
as God's children.

Key scriptures are: John 13:33, 34;
Ephesians 3:14-21; 5:1, 2; 1 John 5:1, 2.

THE CHURCH AS THE TEMPLE OF THE HOLY SPIRIT

The Holy Spirit is the wise master
builder and Christians are living stones
in God's holy temple. Christians are
linked to each other in a holy
community and should live holy lives
in the world.

Key scriptures are: Ephesians 2:21, 22;
1 Peter 2:4-10.

Birds
  Dove The Holy Spirit *Matthew 3:16*,
  Harmless and innocent *Matthew 10:16*,
  Mourners *Isaiah 38:14*
  Eagle God's care of his own
  Exodus 19:4, Renewed strength for
  God's people *Psalm 103:5*

Blindness, blind. Lack of spiritual sight
Isaiah 29:18
Blood Jesus' atoning death
Matthew 26:28; Hebrews 13:20
Body Christ's church *1 Corinthians 12:13*
Book of life Heavenly register of God's
people *Revelation 13:8*
Branch Christ *Isaiah 11:1*
Breastplate Protection for conscience
Ephesians 6:14
Bride The Church *Revelation 21:9*
Burning sulphur Torment
Revelation 14:10

C

Chariots God's authority *Isaiah 66:15*
Crown Delegated authority *Ezekiel 16:12*
Crowns Victorious power *Revelation 9:7*
Cup Blessings of providence and grace
Psalm 16:5, Salvation, grace and mercy
Psalm 116:13, Fellowship; Christ's blood
1 Corinthians 10:16

Symbolic language: D to G

D

Day Appointed season *Isaiah 34:8*, Time of God's grace *1 Corinthians 6:2*, Indefinite period of time with God *2 Peter 3:8*
Death, second. Eternal banishment from God *Revelation 2:11*
Dogs An expression of utter contempt *Matthew 15:26*, Gentiles, outcasts *Matthew 15:27*, People with no conscience *Psalm 22:16*
Drunkenness Worldly excitement *Ephesians 5:18*, Insensibility to judgment *Isaiah 29:9*
Dust Human nature *Genesis 3:19*, Utter humiliation *Psalm 22:15*

E

Earthquake God's power *Job 9:6*, God's presence *Psalm 68:7, 8*, Sign of Christ's coming *Matthew 24:3, 7*, God's judgment *Isaiah 24:19, 20*
Egypt Slavery *Exodus 7-14*, Wickedness *Revelation 11:8*
Eyes Applied to God: Denote his infinite knowledge *Proverbs 15:3*, His providential care *Psalm 32:8*, Applied to Jesus: His omnipresence *Hebrews 4:13* Applied to humans: Understanding *Psalm 119:18*, A friendly counselor *Job 29:15*, Longing for God *Psalm 123:2*

F

Face God's presence *Exodus 33:13-23*, God's favor *Psalm 31:16*, Intelligence *Ezekiel 1:10*, Refusal to repent *Jeremiah 5:3*
Fire Judgment *Matthew 25:41*, Purification *Isaiah 6:6, 7*, God's word being active *Jeremiah 20:8, 9*

FISH

The visible church *Matthew 13:48*, Good followers of God *Matthew 13:48, 49*, Sinners *Matthew 13:48, 49*, People captured by the wicked *Habakkuk 1:14*

There are many images about fishing in the Bible and they are often used in a symbolic way. The Old Testament refers to catching people in nets where the intention of the fishermen is to harm people. By contrast, in the New Testament, Jesus called his followers to fish for men and women. Matthew 4:18, 19 makes it clear that only God can enable his followers to "catch" people for their own good.

The early church favored the symbol of the fish. It was used to identify Christians. The walls of the underground catacombs in Rome have images of fish on them. This was most probably because the Greek word for fish, ichthus, served as a secret acronym, as follows:

Iesous Jesus
Christos Christ
Theou God's
Huios Son
Soter Savior

Forehead Public profession of faith
Revelation 13:14
Forest Kingdom *Jeremiah 21:14*
Foundation Immovable security
2 Timothy 2:19
Furnace Trial and suffering *Jeremiah 11:4*
Divine judgment *Revelation 1:15*

G

Goat Unbelievers *Matthew 25:32, 33*

Gog and Magog God's enemies
Revelation 20:8
Grapes, good Blessings *Amos 9:13*
Grapes, wild Lack of fruitfulness
Isaiah 5:1-7
Grass Uncertainty of life *1 Peter 1:24*,
Wickedness *Isaiah 37:27*, Calamity
Isaiah 15:5, 6, Prosperity of the wicked
Psalm 92:7, God's followers refreshed by
grace *Psalm 72:7; Micah 5:7*

Symbolic language: H to K

H

HANDS

Influence of the Holy Spirit *Ezekiel 8:1,*
Action and service *Psalm 90:17,*
Salvation *Isaiah 59:1*, Right hand.
Protection and favor *Psalm 18:35,*
Laying on of hands. Blessing and
authority *Genesis 48:13-22*

The laying on of hands in both the Old
Testament and the New Testament is a
highly symbolic act. Its meaning is best
understood from the context in which it
takes place.

IDENTIFICATION

Laying on of hands may indicate
identification. This happened in the Old
Testament sacrificial system. Before an
animal sacrifice was killed a person laid
his hands on the animal's head,
Leviticus 4:4, 24.
The idea of identification is continued in
the New Testament as Christians are told
to identify themselves with Jesus, who is
the one who died as a sacrifice for their
sins, Romans 6:1-14.

BLESSING

The way to convey a blessing, Genesis
48:14, was to lay one's hands on the head
of the person who was to receive a
blessing. Jesus did this to children when
he laid his hands on them and blessed
them, Matthew 19:15. Twice in Acts, Acts
8:17; 19:1-7, the apostles laid their hands
on new converts who then received the
Holy Spirit.

HEALING

Sick people had hands laid on them and
were healed, Mark 5:23; Luke 4:40;
Acts 9:12.

ORDINATION

In the Old Testament Levites and priest
were ordained by the laying on of hands,
Leviticus 8:14; Numbers 8:12, and in the
New Testament a similar practice was
adopted for ordination, Acts 6:6; 13:3,
when people were being set apart by God
for a specific form of service.

Hardest stone Hardness of heart
towards God *Ezekiel 3:9*
Harlot: see adulteress
Head Governing principle in people
Isaiah 1:6, Leader *Micah 3:1*, Jesus, as the
head of the Church *Ephesians 1:22*
Heart Emotions, feelings, and affections
Proverbs 6:18; Colossians 3:16

Heavens God's providence *Daniel 4:26,*
Authority and light *Matthew 24:29*, God
Matthew 21:25
Horn, (of Jesus) Salvation *Luke 1:69,*
Power *Jeremiah 48:25*
Hunger and thirst Natural desire for
happiness *Proverbs 19:15; Isaiah 55:1,*
Spiritual desire *Amos 8:11; Matthew 5:6*

I

Incense Devotional exercises
Psalm 141:2; Revelation 5:8
Infants Feeble Christians *1 Corinthians 3:1*

Insects

Ant Wisdom *Proverbs 30:24, 27*, Order
Proverbs 6:7-11
Locusts Horses ready for battle *Joel 2:4;
Revelation 9:7*, Punishment for sin
Deuteronomy 28:38, 42; Joel 1:4, False
teachers and falling away *Revelation 9:3*,
Ungodly rulers *Nahum 3:17*
Moth God's judgments *Isaiah 50:9*,
Corruption *Matthew 6:19, 20*, Human
folly about earthly things *Job 27:18*,
Destruction *James 5:12*
Serpent Deceitfulness *Genesis 3:1*,
Devil *Revelation 12:9*

J

Jerusalem Peace and prosperity
Psalm 122:6, Comfort *Isaiah 66:13*,
Heavenly glory *Revelation 21:22*
Jewels Marks of divine favor *Isaiah 61:10*

K

Keys Power and authority *Revelation 1:18*,
Commission of the gospel ministry
Matthew 16:19

KISS

The significance of a kiss depends on
the relationship between the two
people who kiss. The most common
kiss is a sign of affection between
relatives and friends, Ruth 1:14. In the
context of a ceremony a kiss could be
a sign of respect, 2 Samuel 15:5. To
kiss the hands or feet of a superior
was a sign of submission or worship,
1 Kings 19:18.

In the New Testament Christians
greeted each other with a holy kiss, as
a sign that they belonged to the same
spiritual family, 1 Corinthians 16:20.

Kissing was but one gesture of
hospitality. To bow or prostrate oneself
shows a sign of respect or worship,
Genesis 18:2, 3. A greeting could also
be with words of peace, Luke 10:5, 6,
or by washing a guest's feet, Genesis
18:4; John 13:4, 5, or even by
anointing a person's head, Luke 23:5.

Other gestures included shaking the
dust off one's feet as a sign of
rejection, Luke 9:5, and putting ash on
one's head and tearing one's clothes as
a sign of repentance or strong
emotion, 2 Samuel 13:19, 31;
Luke 10:13.

Jesus used symbolic actions as when he
touched lepers to indicate that he had
power to heal them, Luke 5:12, 13.

Symbolic language: L to P

LIFE

Fullness of joy *Psalm 16:11*, Jesus *John 8:12*

The New Testament speaks about "eternal life" through which Christians are enabled to share God's nature. This eternal life is only found in Jesus Christ who raises the dead and gives them this life, John 5:21-24.

The New Testament has much teaching on eternal life:

Eternal life is a gift from God and is given to all who believe in Jesus. But those who reject Jesus will not see life, John 3:15, 16, 36.

Jesus said that he would give eternal life to those who believe in him, that they would never die or be torn away from him, John 10:10-28.

Jesus himself claimed that he was the resurrection and the life, John 11:1-43.

While our mortal bodies will die, the dead in Christ will rise again and will be immortal, 1 Corinthians 15.

Jesus lives in believers who live by faith in the Son of God, Galatians 2:19, 20.

Believers in Jesus were once dead in their sins but have now been made alive in Christ, not through any merit in themselves, but as a result of God's grace, Ephesians 2:1-10.

Anybody who has the Son has life, while anybody who does not have the Son does not have life, 1 John 5:10-12.

L

Lamb Meek and gentle *Luke 10:3*, Passover. Jesus the sin-bearer *Exodus 12:11; John 1:20*

Lamp Profession of faith *Matthew 25:3, 4*, A Christian church *Revelation 1:12, 20*

Leaf Hypocrisy *Genesis 3:7; Matthew 21:19*, Blessing and healing *Revelation 22:2*

Leprosy Polluted life *Leviticus 13:2*

Light Jesus *John 8:12*, Christians and their testimony *Matthew 5:14, 16*, Holiness *Ephesians 5:8; 1 John 1:7*

Lightning Jesus' second coming
Matthew 24:27

M

Manna Earthly food *Exodus 16:14, 15*,
Spiritual food *John 6:31-35*, Deep spiritual
truths *Revelation 2:17*
Milk Elementary truth from God's Word
1 Corinthians 3:2; 1 Peter 2:2

MOON

In common with other heavenly bodies,
the moon stands for permanence. The
psalmist declares that God's covenant
with David will be established forever,
like the moon, the faithful witness in
the sky, *Psalm 89:37*. The Old
Testament prophets sometimes spoke
about the moon in connection with the
end of history, *Isaiah 13:10; John 2:10;
3:15*. In the New Testament a number
of the passages about the end times
mention the moon which will be
darkened when Jesus comes again,
Matthew 24:29; Mark 13:24; Luke 21:25.

MOTHER

*"Mother" is used in a variety of ways in
the Bible.*

God's compassion: Isaiah alludes to
the maternal instinct when he describes
God's compassion in terms of a mother
comforting her child, *Isaiah 66:13*.

Israel: The nation of Israel is
sometimes described as being like a
mother, *Jeremiah 50:12, 13;
Ezekiel 19:1-14*.

Mustard seed Something small and
insignificant *Matthew 13:31*
Mystery Teaching that remains
unknown until it is revealed
Romans 16:25

N

Naked Devoid of God's righteousness
2 Corinthians 5:3
Nurse Tenderness *Numbers 11:12*

O

Oil Holy Spirit *Psalm 89:20; Matthew 25:1-
13*, Power *Psalm 92:10*, Joy *Isaiah 61:3*,
Healing *Luke 10:34; James 5:14*
Olive, wild Unregenerate humankind
Romans 11:17 ·
Olive, cultivated The Church
Romans 11:24
Owl Solitariness, mourning *Psalm 102:6;
Micah 1:8*

P

Palm tree Reverence, respect *John 12:13*
Paradise Heaven *Luke 23:43*
Passover Jesus' sacrifice for sin
1 Corinthians 5:7
Pillar Mainstay *Galatians 2:9*, The
Church *1 Timothy 3:15*, Monument of
God's grace *Revelation 3:12*
Plumbline Precise measurement,
judgment *Amos 7:7, 8*
Poison Lies, evil principles *Psalm 140:3;
Romans 3:13*
Potter God's gracious sovereignty
Jeremiah 18:1-10
Prostitute: see adulteress
Purple Royalty *Exodus 25:4; John 19:2*

Symbolic language: R to T

R

Ring Honor *Genesis 41:42,*
Royal authority *Esther 3:10,*
Love and friendship *Luke 15:22*
Robe Acceptance *Luke 15:22*

S

Sackcloth Humility *Nehemiah 9:1*
Sand Countless multitudes *Genesis 22:17*
Sapphire Glory of God's throne
Ezekiel 1:26
Scarlet Backsliding *Revelation 17:3, 4*
Scepter Authority, power *Genesis 49:10*
Seal Confirmation *2 Timothy 2:19,*
Sign of special commission *John 6:27*
Shepherd Jesus *John 10:11,* Pastors
Ezekiel 34:2
Sleep Death of a Christian
1 Corinthians 11:30
Smoke Judgment *Revelation 9:2, 3*
Sodom and Gomorrah Backsliding
Isaiah 1:10
Sower Preacher of God's Word
Matthew 13:3, 37
Sparrow God's care, even in small
matters *Psalm 84:3; Matthew 10:29, 31*
Spices Love and care *John 19:39, 40*
Star Prince or ruler *Numbers 24:17*
Sun God's goodness and grace
Psalm 84:11

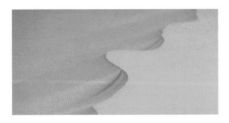

SYMBOLS

The Bible is full of symbols.

Adam: although Adam is an historical
figure, he also symbolizes humankind
who are made in God's image but
disfigured by sin.

Abraham: Abraham is a symbol of a
person who has faith in God and all
who have this are called his children.

Blood: in both the Old Testament and
the New Testament blood symbolizes
an individual's life and Jesus'
substitutionary sacrifice. Whenever the
word "blood" comes in the New
Testament being linked to Jesus it
means Jesus' death.

The cross: the cross is the symbol of
Christianity as it portrays Jesus dying
for the world and the fact that he is
now risen from the dead.

Actions: there are many symbolic
actions recorded in the Bible:

1. Jeremiah bought a field that
belonged to the Babylonians as a sign
that the people of Judah would one day
return.

2. The Lord's Supper was given by Jesus
as a symbolic act portraying the reality
of spiritually partaking of Jesus' body
and blood.

T

Table Fellowship *Psalm 23:5,*
1 Corinthians 10:21
Teeth Cruelty *Proverbs 30:14*
Temple Believer's body
1 Corinthians 3:16, 17; 6:19, 20

Thorns Worldly cares *Luke 8:14*
Throne Earthly kingdom *Genesis 41:40,*
Spiritual kingdom *Colossians 1:16*
Tongue Speech *Proverbs 12:18,*
Remorse and torment *Luke 16:24,*
Mere profession *1 John 3:18*

Topography

Deserts Barrenness *Psalm 106:9, Gentiles Isaiah 35:1, 6*
Desert of Beersheba Refreshment *Genesis 21:14*
Desert of Engedi Place of hiding *1 Samuel 24:1*
Mountains Mountains are sometimes

linked with fertility in the Bible, Deuteronomy 33:15; Jeremiah 50:19. They are also associated with permanence because of their great size, Isaiah 54:10, and with security, 1 Samuel 14:22; Matthew 24:16.

Rivers Rivers are frequently used in a symbolical way, especially in the Old Testament. They illustrate a variety of things: fruitfulness, Psalm 1:3; God's overflowing love, Ezekiel 47; God's judgment, Jeremiah 47:2.

Rocks God as creator *Deuteronomy 31:18*, Christ as foundation *1 Peter 2:6*

MOUNTAINS IN PALESTINE		
Mountain	*Reference*	*Significance in the Bible*
Sinai	Exodus 3:19	God gave the law to Moses
Ebal	Deuteronomy 11:29	Moses is reminded about God's law
Nebo	Deuteronomy 32:49	Place where Moses died
Halak	Joshua 11:17	Southern boundary of Joshua's conquest
Hermon	Joshua 11:17	Northern boundary of Joshua's conquest
Tabor	Judges 4:6	Deborah fought against Sisera
Gilboa	1 Samuel 31:1	Saul killed
Carmel	1 Kings 18:20	Prophets of Baal defeated by Elijah
Zion	Psalm 48:1-2	Site of Old Testament temple
Samaria	Amos 4:1	Capital of the northern kingdom of Israel
Temptation	Luke 4:5	Where Satan tempted Jesus after his baptism
Beatitudes	Matthew 5–7	Site of Jesus' sermon on the mount
Transfiguration	Matthew 17:1	Where Jesus was transfigured
Olives	Matthew 26:30	Gethsemane and site of Jesus' ascension

Symbolic language: V to Y

V

Veil Access to God *Matthew 25:51; Hebrews 9:8*, Obscurity of Mosaic dispensation *2 Corinthians 3:13-16*

VINE

In the Old Testament farming is used to convey a number of spiritual truths, and the picture of the vine and vineyards are often used. Perhaps the most well-known example of this comes in Isaiah 5:1-7 where God is pictured making a vineyard on a fertile hillside. He dug the area over, cleared it of stones, constructed a watchtower and hewed a winepress out of the rock. But the vineyard only produced sour grapes. So all that there is left to do is to allow the vineyard to become a wasteland. See also Psalm 80:8-19.

OTHER AGRICULTURAL IMAGES

Amos 9:13 says that when God establishes his kingdom on earth the reaper will be overtaken by the man ploughing and new wine will drip from the mountains.

Jesus also likened people to trees who produce good or bad fruit, Luke 6:43-45, and Jesus called himself the true vine, John 15:1-8.

Paul used the image of grafting when he explained about the relationship between Gentile and Jewish believers, Romans 11. James points to the example of the farmer who waits for his crops to grow as an illustration of how Christians should exercise patience in their suffering, James 5:7, 8.

Viper Deadly evil *Psalm 140:3*

Virgin Separated from sin, committed to God *2 Corinthians 11:2*

W

Walk Following God's ways *Psalm 1:1*

Wash Moral purification *Psalm 26:6; 73:13*, Spiritual purification *Psalm 51:2; John 3:18*, Pardon and sanctification *1 Corinthians 6:11; Revelation 1:5*

Walls Salvation *Isaiah 26:1*, God's protection *Zechariah 2:5*, Separation *Ephesians 2:14*

WATER

Water is often used in a symbolic way in the Bible. It speaks of:

abundant blessing: God leads his followers to quiet waters where there is plenty of water to drink, Psalm 23:2.

the coming Messiah: when he comes water will pour out into the desert and make streams. The hot sand will be transformed into pools of water, and the thirsty ground will have bubbling springs flowing over it, Isaiah 35:6, 7.

heaven: the book of Revelation ends likening heaven to the river of the water of life which is clear as crystal and which flows from God's throne, Revelation 22:1.

judgment: The Flood brought judgment, Psalm 18:16; 2 Peter 3:6. The idea of water symbolizing judgment is also present in Revelation 8:11 where water becomes polluted.

Wells Salvation *Isaiah 12:3*, The Spirit living in a Christian *John 4:14*
Wheat Genuine profession of faith *Matthew 13:24-30*
Wheels God's providential government *Ezekiel 1:19-21*
White Purity *Mark 16:5; Revelation 1:14*
Widow Being desolate *Isaiah 1:23*

WIND

Wind is used as a symbol for humankind as they chase after the wind, illustrating how mysterious human life is, Ecclesiastes 2:11, 17. Humans are also compared with chaff and smoke which can be blown away in the wind, Psalm 1:4; 18:42; 68:2. While God controls the wind, Psalm 78:26, humans have no idea where the wind (God's Spirit) comes from or where it will go to, John 3:8. In Acts 2:2 the coming of the Holy Spirit on the day of Pentecost is likened to the sound of a violent wind.

Wine Temporal blessing *Psalm 4:7*, Blessing through the gospel *Isaiah 25:6*, God's judgment *Psalm 75:7, 8*
Wings Protection *Psalm 17:8*, Blessing *Malachi 4:2*
Word of God Water *Ephesians 5:26*, Light *Psalm 119:105*, Fire *Jeremiah 20:8, 9*, Hammer *Jeremiah 23:29*, Sword *Hebrews 4:12*, Spiritual food: milk *1 Peter 2:2*, Spiritual food: bread *Matthew 4:4*, Spiritual food: meat *Hebrews 5:12-14*, Spiritual food: honey *Psalm 19:10*
Worm Eternal misery *Mark 9:48*

Y

Yoke Moral restraints *Lamentations 3:27*, Serving Jesus *Matthew 11:29, 30*

The "mystery" truths of Scripture

In the Greek

The Greek word for "mystery" found in the New Testament is *musterion* from which we derive its meaning: to make known special secrets. It refers to what is a temporary secret. Once this is revealed it is understood. God's secret plan of salvation is less clearly seen in the Old Testament than in the New Testament where this "mystery" has been fully revealed.

Hidden from outsiders

The word "mystery" is used concerning what is hidden to outsiders, Mark 4:11. It points to information which has been kept secret, veiled, Romans 16:25, 26.

Significance of "mystery"

This word refers to God's secrets, which include his counsels and purposes. These mysteries can only be known by God's revelation, which is recorded in the Bible, thanks to God's prophets. The only occurrence of the word "mystery" in the Old Testament is in Daniel, 2:18, 19; 27-30; 47: 4:9.

Mystery in the Gospels

In the Gospels, this word only comes three times, Mark 4:11; Matthew 13:11 and Luke 8:10, which are all verses about the same thing. There is a "secret" or "mystery" about the kingdom of heaven. Knowledge of God's kingdom is reserved for those to whom it is given, so to those who are outside it remains hidden in parables. So while the secret of the kingdom of God is preached to everyone, only those with faith will "hear" it and understand the secret.

Mystery in Paul's letters

Apart from the four occurrences of the

word "mystery" in the book of
Revelation, the only other place where
this word occurs is in Paul's letters,
where it is found 21 times. What were
once mysteries, Paul says have now been
revealed.

What are the revealed "mysteries"?

Israel's "hardening" until the complete
number of Gentiles have come in,
Romans 11:25.

Paul's preaching of the gospel,
Romans 16:25.

This mystery was decreed before time
began, 1 Corinthians 2:7.

Paul was commissioned to preach the
secret things of God, 1 Corinthians 4:1.

The mystery about what happens to
Christians after death is explained in
some detail by the apostle Paul in
1 Corinthians 15:51-57.

This mystery was made known to
Paul, Ephesians 1:9, through revelation,
Ephesians 3:3.

Paul says that this mystery was
revealed to the prophets and apostles by
the Spirit, Ephesians 3:5.

This mystery is contained in God's
everlasting counsels and is hidden in
him, Ephesians 3:9.

Paul speaks of Christian marriage in
terms of a profound mystery,
Ephesians 5:32.

The "mystery" is the good news which
is the content of God's revelation,
Ephesians 6:19.

The word of God in its fulness,
Colossians 1:26.

The mystery now disclosed to the
saints, Colossians 1:27.

Christ in you, the hope of glory,
Colossians 1:27.

"...the mystery that has been kept
hidden for ages and generations, but is
now disclosed to the saints. To them
God has chosen to make known among
the Gentiles the glorious riches of this
mystery, which is Christ in you, the
hope of glory" Colossians 1:26, 27.

It is the mystery of God himself, that
is focussed in Christ, Colossians 2:2.

Satan's influence in society,
2 Thessalonians 2:7.

The mystery of godliness,
1 Timothy 3:16.

Paul had been commissioned to
preach about the mystery of the good
news, Ephesians 3:8.

The mystery of the gospel about Jesus
can only be understood in a spiritual
way, Ephesians 3:5.

Bible numbers

One

a. Unity
   i. Unity among Jesus's followers, John 17:21-23; Galatians 3:28; Ephesians 4:4-6
   ii. Unity between Jesus and the Father, John 10:30
   iii. Union between believers and God, John 17:21
b. Uniqueness of God: Deuteronomy 6:4
c. The number one is the number of the unique.
   i. The human race stems from one, Acts 17:26
   ii. The gift of grace comes from one man, Jesus, Romans 5:15
   iii. Christ's sacrificial death is once-for-all, Hebrews 7:27
   iv. Christ is the first-born from among the dead, Colossians 1:18
   v. Christ is the first-fruits from the dead, 1 Corinthians 15:20
d. One expresses single-mindedness: Luke 10:42

Two

a. Two expresses unity
   i. Man and woman form a family unit, Genesis 1:27; 2:20, 24
   ii. Animals go into the ark in pairs, Genesis 7:9
   iii. Two people often work together, Joshua 2:1 (Joshua's spies)
   iv. Jesus sent out the Twelve and the 70 disciples in pairs, Mark 6:7; Luke 10:1
   v. The ten commandments were given on two stone tablets
   vi. Animals were usually offered in pairs
b. Two not only expresses unity, but sometimes it expresses the opposite, disunity, or, separation by force
   i. Limping between two opinions, 1 Kings 18:21
   ii. Jesus spoke about choosing between two ways, Matthew 7:13, 14

Three

a. Godhead, Trinity
   i. Matthew 28:19; John 14:26; 15:26; 2 Corinthians 13;14; 1 Peter 1:2; 1 John 5:7
b. God's mighty deeds
   i. The Lord gave the law on Mount Sinai on the third day, Exodus 19:11
   ii. Hosea prophesied that the Lord would raise up his people on the third day, Hosea 6:2
c. Three sometimes stands for the moment of perfection or completion
   i. Jesus spoke of finishing his work on the third day, Luke 13:32
d. Three sometimes symbolizes something special
   i. Three disciples, Peter, James and John, were allowed to be with Jesus at important moments in his life, Mark 9:2; Matthew 26:37
   ii. On Calvary there were three crosses
   iii. Paul emphasized three virtues, 1 Corinthians 13:13
e. Three sometimes stands for a period

of time

i. David had to choose between three days' pestilence, three months' defeat or three years' famine, 1 Chronicles 21:12

Four

a. Four is one of the numbers that can stand for completion

i. The divine name, Yahweh has four letters in Hebrew: YHWH

ii. Four rivers flowed out of the garden of Eden, Genesis 2:10

iii. There are four corners of the earth, Revelation 7:1; 20:8

iv. Four winds blow from the four corners of the earth, Jeremaih 49:36

v. Ezekiel saw four living creatures in his vision, Ezekiel 1

vi. There are four living creatures in Revelation 4:6

vii. There are four Gospels

b. Four is often used in the apocalyptic books of the Bible

i. Zechariah 1:18-21 has four horns and four craftsmen

ii. The golden altar of Revelation 9:13 has four horns

iii. There are four angels of destruction, Revelation 9:14

Six

a. Six, one short of seven, is the number of humankind

i. On the sixth day God created man and woman, Genesis 1:27

ii. Men and women were to work

for six days, Exodus 20:9

iii. Before a Hebrew servant could be freed he had to work for six years

Seven

a. Seven is the symbolic number for rest, completion, perfection, and fulfilment

i. God rested on the seventh day from his work of creation, Genesis 2:1-3

ii. The seventh day was sanctified by God

iii. Jesus told his followers not just to forgive seven times, but 77 times

b. The Levitical system of feasts was based on a cycle of sevens:

i. Every seventh day there was a Sabbath

ii. Every seventh year a Sabbatical year

iii. Every seventh Sabbatical year was followed by a Year of Jubilee

iv. Every seventh month had three feasts

v. There were seven weeks before Passover and Pentecost

vi. The Day of Atonement was in the seventh month

vii. The Feast of Passover lasted for seven days

viii. The Feast of Tabernacles lasted for seven days

c. Seven is often linked with Old Testament ritual

i. Seven lambs were offered at Pentecost

ii. Bullocks' blood had to be sprinkled seven times, Leviticus 4:6

iii. Seven lambs were offered for a burnt offering, Numbers 28:11

iv. A leper who had been made clean was sprinkled seven times, Leviticus 14:7

v. Naaman was told to dip himself seven times in the River Jordan, 2 Kings 5:10

vi. The candlestick in the temple had seven branches, Exodus 25:32

d. Other notable instances of the number seven include:

i. From the cross Jesus spoke seven times

ii. The priests marched round Jericho seven times, Joshua 6:4

iii. Elijah's servant was sent to look for rain seven times, 1 Kings 18:43

iv. The Psalmist praised God seven times a day, Palm 119:164

v. The early church appointed seven deacons, Acts 6:3

vi. John addresses the seven churches in the book of Revelation

vii. Mary Magdalene was possessed by seven devils

Eight

a. Eight is linked to the resurrection

i. Eight people were "resurrected" from the old, sinful world, who started a new world after the flood, 1 Peter 3:20

ii. Eight people were raised from the dead in the Bible: 1 Kings 17:17-23; 2 Kings 4:32-37; Luke 7:12-15; 8:41-56; John 11:41-44; Acts 9:36-41; 20:9-12

Ten

a. Ten is another number that sometimes stands for completeness

i. Before the flood there were ten patriarchs

ii. There are ten things which cannot separate us from Christ's love, Romans 8:38, 39

   1. death

   2. life

   3. angels

   4. demons

   5. the present

   6. the future

   7. any powers

   8. height

   9. depth

   10. anything else in creation

iii. Ten kinds of people are listed who are excluded from God's kingdom, 1 Corinthians 6:10

   1. the sexually immoral

   2. idolaters

   3. adulterers

   4. male prostitutes

   5. homosexual offenders

   6. thieves

   7. the greedy

   8. drunkards

   9. slanderers

   10. swindlers

iv   Ten elders formed a council,
     Ruth 4:2

12

a. 12 sometimes stands for God's
election
   i.   Israel had 12 sons,
         Genesis 35:22-27; 4:13, 32
  ii. There were 12 tribes of Israel,
         Genesis 49:1-28; Exodus 39:14
 iii. There were 12 apostles, Matthew
         10:2-4. When the number was
         reduced to 11 another person
         was chosen to restore the number
         to 12: Acts 1:15-26

40

a. 40 is linked to nearly all of God's
mighty acts in history, most of which
concern salvation
   i.   Rain for 40 days, Genesis 7:17
  ii. The raven leaves the ark after 40
         days, Genesis 8:6
 iii. Moses fasts for 40 days on Mount
         Sinai, Exodus 24:18
 iv. The spies explore Canaan for 40
         days, Numbers 13:25
  v. Moses prays for Israel for 40
         days, Deuteronomy 9:25
 vi. Goliath defies Israel for 40 days,
         1 Samuel 17:16
 vii. Elijah' journey to Horeb took 40
         days, 1 Kings 19:8
viii. Ezekiel lay on his right side for
         40 days, Ezekiel 4:6 "Lie...on
         your right side...I have asigned
         you 40 days, a day for each
         year."

 ix. Jonah warned Nineveh for 40
         days, Jonah 3:4
  x. Jesus' temptations in the desert
         lasted for 40 days, Matthew 4:2
 xi. Jesus' resurrection appearances
         lasted for 40 days, Acts 1:3

b. The number 40 is sometimes used to
speak of a generation or stand for
something that is complete.
   i.   Moses' life is divided into four
         40-year-long periods, Acts 7:23,
         30, 36, Deuteronomy 31:2
  ii. The Israelites wandered in the
         desert for 40 years, Exodus 16:35
 iii. In the book of Judges God's
         people were often under foreign
         rule for 40 years, Judges 3:11;
         13:2
 iv. Saul, David and Solomon each
         reigned for 40 years, Acts 13:21;
         2 Samuel 5:4; 1 Kings 11:42

70

a. 70 is often associated with God's rule
of the world.
   i.   After the Flood the world was
         repopulated through 70
         descendants of Noah, Genesis 10
  ii. 70 people went down to Egypt,
         Genesis 46:27
 iii. There were 70 elders chosen to
         help Moses look after Israel in
         the desert, Numbers 11:16
 iv. The people of Judah spent 70
         years in exile in Babylon,
         Jeremiah 25:11
  v. Jesus sent out 70 disciples to
         preach and heal, Luke 10:1

Symbols and numbers in the book of Revelation

Symbolic words in Revelation

Rainbow

The rainbow of 4:3 surrounds God's throne in heaven and stands for the majesty of God.

Four horses

The four horses and four horsemen of 6:2-8 refers back to the imagery of Zechariah 1:8-17; 6:1-8. The four colors of the horses in the book of Revelation refer to the characters of the riders.

- The white horse stands for conquest.
- The fiery red horse stands for war and bloodshed.
- The black horse symbolizes famine.
- The pale horse stands for death.

A Lamb

"Then I saw a Lamb, looking as if it had been slain, standing in the center of the throne, encircled by the four living creatures and the elders" 5:6. Here the Lamb is seen as the sacrifice for sin, see Isaiah 53:7; John 1:29; Hebrews 9:1-28; 1 Corinthians 5:7; 1 Peter 1:18, 19.

The book of Revelation uses a special word for "lamb" and comes 29 times in this book. A different word for lamb is used elsewhere in the New Testament, except in John 21:15.

But in 17:14 the Lamb is pictured as the mighty conqueror. "The Lamb is... Lord of lords and King of kings."

Wormwood

"Wormwood" 8:11 means "bitterness" and stands for sorrow and calamity.

Babylon

In chapters 18 and 19 the fall of Babylon is described in great detail. Babylon stands for the world opposed to God.

Sodom

"Sodom" in 11:8 stands for the low morality of the "great city" which is under discussion.

Egypt

"Egypt," also mentioned in 11:8, stands for slavery and oppression.

Armageddon

"Armageddon," 16:16, is symbolic for God finally overthrowing evil, and need not stand for any specific geographic location.

Two witnesses

The "two witnesses" of 11:3 are usually taken to refer to Moses and Elijah and so to believers who give faithful witness to God in the final time before Christ's return.

Names of Jesus

There are 30 names, titles, and actions attributed to Jesus Christ which each speak of some facet of his divine character.

1. Jesus Christ 1:1
2. Faithful witness 1:5
3. The firstborn from the dead 1:5
4. The ruler of the kings of the earth 1:5

5. The one who has "freed us from our sins" 1:5
6. The Alpha and the Omega 1:8: the first and last letters of the Greek alphabet, standing for Jesus' sovereignty.
7. Lord 1:8
8. The Almighty 1:8: out of the 12 times this word comes in the New Testament there are nine occurrences of it in the book of Revelation.
9. Son of man 1:13
10. The First and the Last 1:17: the same as the "Alpha and the Omega" of 1:8; 21:6.
11. The Living One 1:18: as Jesus has conquered death he is called the Living One, see Romans 6:9.
12. The Son of God 2:18
13. Holy and true 3:7: in 1 John 2:20 and 1 John 5:20 these two titles are used separately to refer to God, and in Revelation 6:10 they come together to refer to God.
14. The Amen 3:14
15. The ruler of God's creation 3:14
16. The one who "created all things" 4:11
17. The Lion of the tribe of Judah 5:5
18. The Root of David 5:5: in Isaiah 11:10 the future prince from the house of David is called "the Root of Jesse."
19. Lamb 5:6
20. The one who "will reign for ever and ever" 11:15: God's sovereignty has never been in doubt, but now it will

be universally acknowledged.
21. A male child 12:5: refers to Jesus being the Messiah
22. "Who will rule all the nations" 12:5
23. Christ 12:10
24. Jesus 14:12
25. Lord of lords 17:14: Jesus' overwhelming sovereignty is emphasized by this title and the next one. See also Deuteronomy 10:17; Psalm 136:2, 3; Daniel 2:47; 1 Timothy 6:15.
26. King of kings 17:14
27. The Word of God 19:13: this is a clear echo of John 1:1-14
28. The Beginning and the End 22:13: this verse combines 1:8, 17 and 21:6.
29. The bright Morning Star 22:16: this is a reference to Balaam's prophecy found in Numbers 14:17, which refers to David and his conquests, and so, by extension to David's great Son, Jesus.
30. Lord Jesus 22:20

666

"If anyone has insight, let him calculate the number of the beast, for it is a man's number. His number is 666" Revelation 13:18.

It is clear from this verse that 666 stands for a person, "for it is a man's number." But exactly to whom it refers is still debated.

One possibility relies on that fact that in Hebrew and in Greek the letters of the alphabet stand also for numerals. So a numerical value can be given to any word. Also any number may be a code for a particular word. For example there is a Greek graffito that has been unearthed at Pompeii which reads, "I love the girl whose number is 545."

Using this scheme, the sum of the letters of the word Nero-Caesar when written in Hebrew produces the total of 666. But if you work with the Greek for 666 it gives the word "Titus" who could refer to the third Roman Emperor, Titus Domitian.

Other schemes used to decode 666 have produced a variety of names, such as Euanthas, Lateinos, and Nero Caesar.

Some commentators have pointed out that 666 may stand for a trinity of imperfection and evil, as each digit falls short of the perfect number 7.

As it was a time of persecution the writer of the book of Revelation often used codes which would have been clear to his first Christian readers, but would have baffled other readers, as it does us today.

For the number seven in the book of Revelation see page 121.

144,000

"Then I looked, and there before me was the Lamb, standing on Mount Zion, and with him 144,000 who had his name and his Father's name written on their foreheads" Revelation 14:1. See also Revelation 7:3.

144,000 is the number 12, the number of the elected, squared and then multiplied by 1,000 (which stands for an indefinitely large number). 12 x 12 x 1,000 = 144,000.

So 144,000 symbolizes the complete number of God's people who are preserved by God.